D1551485

Бжⷭ҇твенныѧ литꙋргі́и
ста́гѡ а҆пⷭ҇тола і҆а́кѡва
бра́та гдⷵнѧ

The Divine Liturgies
of the Holy Apostle James
Brother of the Lord

И҆зда́тельство
Свѧто-Тро́ицкагѡ Монастырѧ.
тѷпогра́фїѧ преп. І҆́ѡва Поча́евскагѡ.
Джорданвѝль, Н.І.̈

2020

Printed with the blessing of His Eminence,
Metropolitan Hilarion, First Hierarch
of the Russian Orthodox Church Outside of Russia

The Divine Liturgies of the Holy Apostle James,
Brother of the Lord: Slavonic-English Parallel Text
© 2020 Holy Trinity Monastery

Text of the Troparion and Kontakion
for St James © 2007 Reader Isaac E. Lambertsen

The Church Slavonic text of the Liturgy of St James,
translated by Philip (Ivan Alexeyevich) Gardner, and the
Church Slavonic text of the Presanctified Liturgy of St
James, translated by the Most Rev. Bishop Jerome (Shaw),
were revised and augmented by Vitaly Permiakov

English translation and Preface by Vitaly Permiakov.

PRINTSHOP OF
SAINT JOB OF POCHAEV

An imprint of

HOLY TRINITY PUBLICATIONS
Holy Trinity Monastery
Jordanville, New York 13361-0036
www.holytrinitypublications.com

ISBN: 978-0-88465-430-8

Library of Congress Control Number 2019940214

TABLE OF CONTENTS

Тропа́рь, гла́съ в҃:

Ꙗ҆́кѡ гдⷵень оу҆чнⷭ҇и́къ, воспрїа́лъ є҆сѝ пра́ведне є҆ѵⷢ҇лїе: ꙗ҆́кѡ мчⷭ҇нкъ и҆́маши, є҆́же неѡпи́санное, дерзнове́нїе, ꙗ҆́кѡ бра́тъ бж҃їй, є҆́же моли́тисѧ, ꙗ҆́кѡ і҆ера́рхъ. молѝ хрⷭ҇та̀ бг҃а, спасти́сѧ дꙋша́мъ на́шымъ.

Конда́къ, гла́съ д҃:

Ѻ҆́чее є҆диноро́дное бг҃ъ сло́во, прише́дшее къ на́мъ въ послѣ̑днѧѧ дни̑, ꙗ҆́кѡве бж҃твенне, пе́рваго тѧ̀ показа̀ і҆ерꙋсали́млѧнъ па́стырѧ и҆ оу҆чи́телѧ, и҆ вѣ́рнаго строи́телѧ та́инствъ дꙋхо́вныхъ: тѣ́мже тѧ̀ всѝ чти́мъ, а҆пⷭ҇толе.

Troparion, Tone II

As a disciple of the Lord thou didst receive the Gospel, O just one; as a martyr thou dost possess what is infinite; as the brother of God, thou hast boldness before Him; and as a hierarch, thou canst make entreaty. Beseech Christ God, that our souls be saved.

Kontakion, Tone IV

The Word of God, the Only-begotten of the Father, Who came unto us in latter times, showed thee to be the first pastor and teacher of the people of Jerusalem, and a faithful server of the mysteries of the Spirit, O godly James. Wherefore, we all honor thee, O apostle.

Fresco of the Apostle James Brother of the Lord,
Holy Trinity Cathedral, Jordanville, New York.

PREFACE

This volume represents the first bilingual Church Slavonic-English edition of the Divine Liturgy of St James, as well as the first bilingual edition of the Divine Liturgy of the Presanctified Gifts, also attributed to the same author. According to the testimony of the New Testament and the ecclesiastical tradition, the holy apostle James, the brother of the Lord (*adelphotheos*), was one of the first eyewitnesses to the resurrection of Christ (1 Cor 15:7) and the early leader of the Christian Church of Jerusalem who presided at the Council of Jerusalem (Acts 15) and composed the Epistle of James. Later Byzantine tradition named St James as the first bishop of Jerusalem and the legendary author of the earliest eucharistic liturgy (*Synaxarion of Constantinople*). However, aside from the testimony of the New Testament and two short prayers in the late first century *Didache* (*The Teaching of the Twelve Apostles*),

no authentic liturgical texts of the apostolic or post-apostolic period survive to this day.

The Divine Liturgy and the Presanctified Liturgy attributed to St James were at the center of the liturgical life in the Holy City of Jerusalem and in the Orthodox Patriarchate of Jerusalem before the end of the first millennium AD. The attribution of these liturgies to the holy apostle James is based on the fact that these liturgies were the integral components of the ancient liturgical tradition of Jerusalem, i.e. the local Orthodox church that acclaimed St James as its first ruling bishop. In the course of several centuries since the establishment of Jerusalem as a Christian city and the construction of the Church of the Holy Sepulcher (AD 325–335), the prayers of this liturgy were composed, developed, and assembled under the authority of the holy hierarchs and successors of St James, who presided over the church in the Holy City, celebrated the eucharist in the Holy Sepulcher (the site of the Lord's Tomb), on Golgotha, in the now-lost basilica of Holy Sion (the place of the Last Supper), in Bethlehem, on the Mount of Olives, and in every holy place associated with the life, death, and resurrection of our Lord Jesus Christ. This is the

liturgy which was most likely celebrated and prayed by many saints of the Jerusalem Church who are loved and honored by all Orthodox faithful: St Cyril of Jerusalem (d. 387), St Euthymius (d. 473), St Sabas (d. 532), St Sophronius (d. 638), St John of Damascus (d. 750), St Kosmas of Mayuma (d. 760), St John Climacus (d. 649), St Anastasius of Sinai (d.c. 700), and other bishops, priests, and monks who served the Lord in Jerusalem, Palestine, Mt Sinai, and in the Orthodox Church of Georgia (until the 12th century). Many of those saintly hierarchs and priests of the Jerusalem Church are commemorated in this liturgy during the holy anaphora, and in both liturgies the Church prays for the Holy City, for the Orthodox Church in that city that serves the Lord in the place where our salvation has come to pass.

Divine Liturgy of St James[1]

It is likely that the liturgy mentioned and quoted by St Cyril of Jerusalem (d. 387) in his *Mystagogical Catecheses* (*Cat.* 5) may have been an early form of

---

[1]This section of the preface is indebted to the research of such liturgical scholars, as Heinzgerd Brakmann, Tinatin Chronz, Fr Michael Zheltov, Daniel Galadza, and others.

the Jerusalem liturgy, now known as the Liturgy of St James. As it remained the main eucharistic liturgy of the city of Jerusalem, Palestine, Mount Sinai, Georgia until the eleventh-twelfth centuries, the Liturgy of St James continued to evolve and expand. The earliest Greek manuscripts containing the text of this liturgy are attributed to the eighth-tenth centuries AD. Some of the most important early witnesses to the text of the liturgy include the eighth/ninth cent. ms. *Sinai Greek NE MG 118* (from the New Finds collection of St Catherine's Monastery on Sinai), ms. *Vatican Greek 2282* (9th cent., from Antioch), *Messina Greek 177* (11th cent.), *Vatican Greek 1970* (13th cent.), and others. Because the Georgian Orthodox Church celebrated the Liturgy of St James until the 12th-13th century, liturgical scholars attribute special importance to the Georgian translations of the Liturgy of St James, and to Georgian manuscript witnesses, including *Tbilisi A 86* (11th cent.), *Sinai Georgian 12, 53, 54*, and several manuscripts from the Sinai New Finds collection. Medieval liturgical manuscripts, including those containing the Liturgy of St James, usually included for the most part just the text and inscriptions of

priestly prayers and diaconal litanies, but no detailed rubrics that would describe liturgical actions of the clergy (e.g. entrances). For the Byzantine service books, such expansion of the uniform detailed rubrics became a standard feature with the Diataxis of Patriarch Philotheos Kokkinos, composed in mid-14th century. This development never affected the Jerusalem rite and its eucharistic liturgy, the Liturgy of St James, since by that time its celebration had largely ceased across the Orthodox world.

The first printed edition of the Greek text of the Liturgy of St James was published in Paris in 1560 on the basis of only one late manuscript—the 16th century *Paris Suppl. gr. 303*. It is this edition, based on a single late manuscript, which was used in 1886 by Dionysios II (Latas), Archbishop of Zakynthos (1835–1894) for the publication of a new Greek edition of the Liturgy of St James, specifically designed for liturgical use. In this edition, Archbishop Dionysios did not only seek to republish the known text of this liturgy, but to revise the text in accordance with his own ideas concerning the "ancient" form of liturgical celebration. For this reason, the 1886 edition introduced the usages now perceived

as unique and distinctive within the Liturgy of St James: deacon's chanting the litanies while facing the people, and the peculiar and fanciful order of the Scripture readings (Old Testament—Gospel—Epistle). The original manuscripts for the Liturgy of St James, however, do not mention anything about deacon's orientation during litanies. The lectionary sources for the rite of Jerusalem in the 5th-8th centuries indeed prescribe Old Testament readings for some (but not all) feast days, but the traditional order of the readings for Jerusalem resembles that of the Byzantine rite: prokeimenon—[Old Testament, if appointed]—Epistle— Alleluia—Gospel. This is the order which is restored in this bilingual edition.

Translations of the full text of the Liturgy of St James into Church Slavonic appeared rather late, in a few of the 16th-17th century manuscripts, where they were unlikely to have been meant for liturgical use. In 1936 the renowned Russian Orthodox musicologist, Hegumen Philip (Ivan Alexeyevich) Gardner (1898–1984), produced in Jerusalem his own new translation of the liturgy into Church Slavonic and composed the complete new set of rubrics for hierarchal and presbyteral celebration

of this liturgy. The sources for Gardner's translation and rubrics were the 1886 edition of St James' Liturgy by Archbishop Dionysios (Latas), the 1912 Jerusalem edition by Chrysostomos Papadopoulos, and Gardner's own observations at the celebration of this liturgy by Patriarch Timothy I of Jerusalem on November 5, 1936. For this reason, apparently, Gardner's rubrics for the Liturgy of St James included some specific Greek Orthodox usages, such as the performance of entrances through the entire nave of the church, etc.

In 1938, Gardner's translation of the Liturgy of St James was published in Ladomirová (Slovakia) by the Brotherhood of St Job of Pochaev. Even before that, on January 18/31, 1938, with a blessing of the First Hierarch of the Russian Church Abroad, Metropolitan Anastasy (Gribanovsky), Fr Philip celebrated this liturgy for the first time in the Russian Church of the Holy Trinity in Belgrade. Since that time, the rubrics of the Gardner edition became the standard way of celebrating the Liturgy of St James in the Russian Orthodox Church Outside of Russia and (since the late 1960s) in the Russian Orthodox Church. In the churches of the Greek tradition, the

celebration of the Liturgy of St James relies upon the 1912 Jerusalem edition, as well as on more recent editions, such as the edition by Prof. Ioannis Phountoulis (Thessalonica, 1977). Thus, both the contemporary Greek and Russian traditions of celebrating the Liturgy of St James are based upon the renewal and (in some ways) reinvention of this liturgy by Archbishop Dionysios (Latas) in 1880s.

However, the current state of scholarship on the Liturgy of St James relies on a wider range of liturgical sources, including the Sinai New Finds, as well as on a more profound understanding of the history of the liturgy in Jerusalem during the first millennium. In 2006 Alkiviades Kazamias published a new critical edition of the Liturgy of St James, which expanded and updated the previous critical edition by B.-Ch. Mercier in 1946. In 2011 a group of Georgian scholars produced a critical edition of the Old Georgian text of St James' Liturgy, which reflects in some parts the older recension of the text of the liturgy. Both the 2006 and the 2011 edition have been used in the preparation of this bilingual Church Slavonic/ English edition of the Liturgy of St James.

Liturgy of the Presanctified Gifts of St James

The existence of the Liturgy of the Presanctified
Gifts as part of the ancient rite of the Orthodox
Church of Jerusalem is clearly attested in the sources:
the ms. *Sinai Greek 1040* (12th cent.), a few of the
Georgian euchologion manuscripts, reflecting the
Jerusalem tradition, and the so-called "Typicon of
the Anastasis" (ms. *Hagiou Stavrou 43*, 1122 AD).
However, only the diaconal litanies have survived
in the original Greek, while the priestly prayers have
been preserved in the Georgian translation. Likewise, the manuscripts which include the prayers of
the Presanctified Liturgy do not include the prayers
for the Jerusalem-rite Vespers. Thus, the preparation
of the text of the Presanctified Liturgy of St James
which is suitable for liturgical use in the contemporary Orthodox setting requires the work of careful
restoration, based on the current state of liturgical
scholarship.

   The first reconstruction of the full text of the
Presanctified Liturgy of St James has been accom-
plished by Professor Ioannis Phountoulis (Thessalonica, 1979) who combined the extant text of the
diaconal litanies with the prayers taken from the full

Liturgy of St James, while ignoring the witness of the Georgian manuscripts. In the 2000s, Phountoulis' edition was translated into the Church Slavonic by the Most Revd Bishop Jerome (Shaw).

In the current edition, the priestly prayers of the communion part of the Presanctified Liturgy of St James have been translated from the Old Georgian, as found in the 1950 edition of the Jerusalem liturgies by Michael Tarchnishvili. The prayers of the vesperal part of the liturgy have been translated from the earliest Greek Palestinian euchologion *Sinai NE MΓ 53* (8th-9th cent.). As in the first reconstruction of this liturgy by Phountoulis, the prayers for the catechumens at the end of the Vesperal part were translated from the so-called "Typicon of the Anastasis," with the exception of the last prayer—for those preparing for baptism—which was appropriated from the Jerusalem rite of baptism in the Old Georgian euchologion *Sinai Georgian 12* (11th cent.).

This Edition

This bilingual edition of the two Jerusalem liturgies, traditionally attributed to the holy apostle James, intends to supply the Orthodox clergy and

the faithful with the text of these two liturgies that is both faithful to the tradition of this liturgy as it is reflected in the most important manuscripts and is suitable for liturgical use. In view of these objectives, the preparation of this volume involved a careful and painstaking comparison and analysis of the Greek, Georgian, and Church Slavonic texts of these liturgies, relying upon the existing critical editions and the liturgical scholarship.

Specific changes in the order of the Liturgy of St James that have been introduced in this present edition include the following:

1) this edition eliminates the rubric based on Archbishop Dionysios Latas' 1886 edition, which prescribed the deacon to face west (the people) while chanting the litanies; following the traditional liturgical practice of the Orthodox Church, the deacon is directed to face east in this edition;

2) as noted above, the order of Scripture readings have been restored to conform with the witness of the Jerusalem Lectionary (5th-8th cent.) and the traditional order of readings observed in the Orthodox Church; likewise, the directions concerning the

procession to the middle of the nave for the Scripture readings have been removed;

3) in accordance with the witness of the Jerusalem Tropologion (before 8th cent.) and the Georgian manuscripts of the Liturgy of St James, the *handwashing hymn* (стихира на умовеніе рукъ) has been restored in its original place before the hymn for the transfer of the gifts (in this book, the hymn "Let all mortal flesh keep silence . . .");

4) the extended commemoration list of the Saints at the end of the anaphora that appeared in most ancient Greek manuscripts of the Liturgy, but omitted in the most 19th-20th century editions of this liturgy, has been restored to its original place;

5) the detailed rubric describing the manual acts preceding the clergy communion in the Liturgy of St James has been removed, as it is difficult to follow for the clergy of the contemporary Orthodox churches; instead, for the fraction of the Lamb, the clergy is directed to follow the customary usage of the Liturgies of St John Chrysostom and St Basil. Likewise, on other occasions, when a particular liturgical action did not differ significantly from the use of the Byzantine rite, the rubric was supplied

from the received Service Book (Служебникъ) of the Orthodox Church;

6) for the communion of the laity, the present edition prescribes the customary practice for the Orthodox churches, i.e. communion with a liturgical spoon; no ancient manuscripts of the Liturgy of St James mention anything about the laity receiving communion under both kinds separately—the latter was a common usage in the Orthodox churches before the 10th-11th centuries, and does not represent the custom specific to the Liturgy of St James;

7) the prayer in the diakonikon after the dismissal was translated from the 2006 edition of the Greek Liturgy of St James (p. 223), while the prayer before the consuming of the gifts has been translated from the Old Georgian, as found in the 2011 edition of the Georgian recension of this liturgy (p. 140).

Throughout the text of both liturgies, whenever the priest is expected to make a sign of the Cross over the diskos or the chalice, the sign of the Cross (✠) appears in the rubric or in the text of the prayer.

The Church Slavonic text for the Liturgy of St James uses for the most part Philip Gardner's translation which was revised after the older Slavonic

translations of St James's Liturgy (see Syrku, 1890) while some of the prayers were translated anew from the Greek or the Georgian. The Church Slavonic text for the Presanctified Liturgy of St James is a revised translation by the Most Revd Bishop Jerome, with some prayers freshly translated from the Georgian. The English translation of both liturgies was done from the extant original text, Greek or Georgian.

This edition would not have been possible without the encouragement and blessing of the Most Revd Luke, Bishop of Syracuse and Abbot of Holy Trinity Monastery, and the attention and assistance of the management and the editorial staff of Holy Trinity Publications, especially Nicholas & Nina Chapman and Protodeacon Peter Markevich. Special thanks is due to all those who encouraged, supported, and in any way assisted this publication, especially the Most Revd Bishop Jerome (Shaw), Hieromonk Herman (Majkrzak) of St Tikhon's Monastery, and Daniel Galadza.

This bilingual edition has been prepared for the benefit and edification of Orthodox Christian clergy and the faithful, in the hope that they, perusing and praying the words of this ancient liturgy, may be

brought to a greater and deeper understanding of the liturgical heritage of the Orthodox Church and that we all may be encouraged to be not only "hearers," but "doers" of the inspired sacred words (James 1:22).

—Vitaly Permiakov
Feast of St Jonah, Metropolitan of Moscow
June 15/28, 2019

Бжⷭ҇твеннаѧ лїтꙋргі́а ст҃а́гѡ сла́внагѡ а҆пⷭ҇ла і҆а́кѡва, бра́та гдⷭ҇нѧ, пе́рвагѡ є҆пⷭ҇іскопа і҆ерⷭ҇ли́мскагѡ.

Вре́мени пришѐдшꙋ нача́ти бжⷭ҇твеннꙋю слꙋ́жбꙋ, и҆схо́дитъ дїа́конъ и҆́зъ ст҃а́гѡ Ѻ҆лтарѧ̀ и҆ ста́нетъ на ю́жной странѣ̀ ст҃ы́хъ двере́й, зрѧ́ще къ восто́кꙋ. А҆́ще сꙋ́ть мно́зїи дїа́коны, и҆схо́дѧтъ и҆ ста́нꙋтъ по Ѻ҆бою странꙋ̀ ст҃ы́хъ двере́й, два̀ два̀, зрѧ́ще къ восто́кꙋ. Сщ҃е́нникъ же пред̾ ст҃о́ю трапе́зою гл҃етъ мл҃твꙋ сїю̀, ти́химъ гла́сомъ, ѡ҆ себѣ̀ самѣ́мъ оу҆молѧ́юще:

Во мно́жествѣ грѣхѡ́въ ѡ҆скверне́ннаго мѧ̀, да не оу҆ничижи́ши, влⷣко гдⷭ҇и бж҃е мо́й: се бо приходѧ́й къ бжⷭ҇твенномꙋ семꙋ̀ и҆ небе́сномꙋ же́ртвенникꙋ, не ꙗ҆́кѡ досто́инъ сы́й дерза́ю, но на твою̀ взира́ю бл҃гость,

THE DIVINE LITURGY OF THE HOLY GLORIOUS APOSTLE JAMES, THE BROTHER OF THE LORD AND THE FIRST BISHOP OF JERUSALEM

When the time to begin the divine service has come, the deacon goes out of the holy altar and stands to the south of the holy doors, looking toward the east. If there are many deacons, they go out and stand on both sides of the holy doors, two by two, looking to the east. The priest before the holy table, in a quiet voice, says this prayer entreating for himself:

Defiled though I am by a multitude of sins, reject me not utterly, O Master, Lord my God; for behold, I draw near to this divine and heavenly altar, not as though I were worthy, but looking up to Thy goodness,

се́й и҆спꙋща́ю гла́съ: бж҃е ми́лостивъ бꙋ́ди
мѝ грѣ́шномꙋ, согрѣши́хъ бо на не́бо и҆
пред̾ тобо́ю, и҆ нѣ́смь досто́инъ воззрѣ́ти
на сщ҃е́ннꙋю сїю̀ и҆ дх҃о́внꙋю трапе́зꙋ, на
не́йже є҆диноро́дный тво́й сн҃ъ, гдⷭ҇ь и҆ бг҃ъ
на́шъ і҆и҃съ хрⷭ҇то́съ, мно́ю грѣ́шнымъ и҆ во
всꙗ́кой скве́рнѣ ѡ҆калꙗ́ннымъ, та́йнѡ
предлага́етсꙗ въ же́ртвꙋ. Сего̀ ра́ди сїѐ тебѣ̀
моле́нїе прино́шꙋ, во є҆́же ниспосла́ти
дх҃а тво́егѡ оу҆тѣ́шителѧ, оу҆крѣплꙗ́юща и҆
оу҆твержда́юща мѧ̀ во слꙋ́жбѣ се́й, и҆ ѿ
тебѣ̀ возвѣще́нный мѝ гла́съ неѡсꙋжде́ннѡ
лю́демъ проповѣ́дати сподо́би, ѡ҆ хрⷭ҇тѣ̀ і҆и҃сѣ
гдⷭ҇ѣ на́шемъ, съ ни́мже бл҃гослове́нъ є҆сѝ,
со престы́мъ и҆ бл҃ги́мъ и҆ животворꙗ́щимъ
тво́имъ дх҃омъ, ны́нѣ и҆ при́снѡ и҆ во вѣ́ки
вѣкѡ́въ, а҆ми́нь.

Ѿверза́етсꙗ завѣ́са и҆ ст҃ы̑ѧ две́ри,
дїа́конъ же ста́въ пред̾ ст҃ы́ми двермѝ
глаго́летъ:

Го́споди, бл҃гословѝ.

Сщ҃е́нникъ же возглаша́етъ:

I raise my voice unto Thee: O God, be merciful to me, a sinner! For I have sinned before heaven and before Thee, and I am not worthy to gaze upon this sacred and spiritual table, on which Thine only-begotten Son, our Lord Jesus Christ, is mystically set forth as a sacrifice by me a sinner, who is stained by every defilement. Therefore, I bring forth this entreaty to Thee, to send me Thy Spirit, the Comforter, to strengthen and fortify me for this liturgy, and vouchsafe that I may without condemnation proclaim to the people this word that has been announced unto me, in Christ Jesus our Lord, with whom Thou art blessed and glorified, together with Thine All-holy, good, and life-giving Spirit, now and ever and unto the ages of ages. Amen.

The curtain and the holy doors are opened, and the deacon stands before the holy doors and says:

Lord, bless.

And the priest exclaims:

Сла́ва ѻ҆ц҃ꙋ̀ и҆ сн҃ꙋ и҆ ст҃о́мꙋ дх҃ꙋ, трѻи́чномꙋ и҆ є҆ди́нственномꙋ свѣ́тꙋ є҆ди́нагѡ бж҃ества, и҆́же въ трⷯцѣ є҆ди́нственнѣ сꙋщагѡ и҆ раздѣ́ла́емагѡ нераздѣ́льнѣ: трⷪ҇ца во є҆ди́нъ бг҃ъ вседержи́тель, є҆гѡ́же сла́вꙋ небеса̀ повѣ́даютъ, зе́млѧ̀ же тогѡ̀ вла́чество, мо́ре тогѡ̀ держа́вꙋ, и҆ всѧ̀ чꙋ́вст= венна́ѧ же и҆ оу҆́мна́ѧ тва́рь тогѡ̀ вели́чество проповѣ́дꙋютъ, всегда̀, ны́нѣ и҆ при́снѡ и҆ во вѣ́ки вѣкѡ́въ.

Ли́къ: а҆ми́нь.
Дїа́конъ: гдⷣꙋ помо́лимсѧ.
Ли́къ: гдⷣи, поми́лꙋй.

Сщ҃е́нникъ гл҃етъ мл҃твꙋ сїю̀ возгла́снѡ:

Бл҃годѣ́телю, и҆ цр҃ю̀ вѣкѡ́въ и҆ тва́ри всѧ́кїѧ содѣ́телю, прїимѝ приходѧ́щꙋю къ тебѣ̀ хрⷭ҇то́мъ твои́мъ цр҃ковь твою̀, и҆ коемꙋ́ждо поле́зное и҆спо́лни, приведи́ же всѣ́хъ въ соверше́нїе и҆ досто́йны на́съ содѣ́лай бл҃года́ти ѡ҆сще́нїѧ твоегѡ̀, собра́въ на́съ во ст҃ꙋ́ю свою̀ собо́рнꙋю и҆ а҆пⷭ҇льскꙋ́ю

Glory to the Father, and to the Son, and to the Holy Spirit, the triadic and unique Light of the one divinity, abiding singly in the Trinity and indivisibly divided: for the Trinity is one God almighty, whose glory the heavens proclaim, and the earth His lordship, and the sea His dominion, and every sensible and spiritual creature proclaims His majesty, always, now and ever and unto the ages of ages.

SINGERS: Amen.

DEACON: Let us pray to the Lord.

SINGERS: Lord, have mercy.

The priest says this prayer aloud:

O Benefactor, King of the ages and Fashioner of every creature, receive thy Church that comes forth to Thee through Thy Christ, and fulfill that which is profitable for each, bring all to perfection, and make us worthy of the grace of Thy sanctification, gathering us together in Thy holy, catholic, and

цр҃ковь, ю҆́же стѧжа́лъ є҆сѝ чт҃но́ю кро́вїю
є҆диноро́днагѡ твоегѡ̀ сн҃а, гда̀ же и҆ сп҃са
на́шегѡ і҆и҃са хр҃та̀, съ ни́мже бл҃гослове́нъ є҆сѝ,
со прест҃ы́мъ и҆ бл҃гимъ и҆ животворѧ́щимъ
твои́мъ дх҃омъ, нн҃ѣ и҆ при́снѡ и҆ во вѣ́ки
вѣкѡ́въ.

Ли́къ: а҆ми́нь.

Сщ҃е́нникъ: Ми́ръ всѣ́мъ.

Ли́къ: И҆ дꙋ́хови твоемꙋ̀.

Дїа́конъ: Гд҃ꙋ помо́лимсѧ.

Ли́къ: Гд҃и, поми́лꙋй.

Сщ҃е́нникъ бл҃гословлѧ́етъ кади́льницꙋ и҆
глаго́летъ мл҃твꙋ кади́ла, на вхо́дъ:

Бж҃е, прїе́млѧй а҆́велевы да́ры, но́евꙋ и҆
а҆враа́мовꙋ же́ртвꙋ, а҆арѡ́ново и҆ заха́рїино
кади́ло: прїимѝ и҆ ѿ рꙋ́къ на́съ грѣ́шныхъ
кади́ло сїѐ, въ воню̀ бл҃гоꙋха́нїѧ и҆ во
ѡ҆ставле́нїе грѣхѡ́въ на́шихъ и҆ всѣ́хъ люде́й
твои́хъ, и҆ сотворѝ со вхо́домъ на́шимъ
вхо́дꙋ ст҃ы́хъ а҆́гг҃лѡвъ бы́ти, сослꙋжа́щихъ
съ на́ми твое́й бл҃гости. Ꙗ҆́кѡ бл҃гослове́нъ

apostolic Church, which Thou hast obtained by the precious blood of Thine only-begotten Son, our Lord and Saviour Jesus Christ, with whom Thou art blessed with Thine All-holy, good, and life-giving Spirit, now and ever, and unto the ages of ages.

SINGERS: Amen.

PRIEST: Peace be unto all.

SINGERS: And to thy spirit.

DEACON: Let us pray to the Lord.

SINGERS: Lord, have mercy.

The priest blesses the incense and says this prayer of incense, for the entrance:

O God who didst receive the gifts of Abel, the sacrifice of Noah and Abraham, the incense of Aaron and Zacharias: Receive also this incense from the hands of us sinners as an odor of good fragrance for the remission of our sins and of all Thy people, and grant that with our entrance there may be an entrance of holy angels, serving and ministering with

є҆сѝ, и҆ подоба́етⸯ тѝ сла́ва, ѻ҆ц҃ꙋ, и҆ сн҃ꙋ, и҆ ст҃о́мꙋ дх҃ꙋ, ны́нѣ и҆ при́снѡ и҆ во вѣ́ки вѣкѡ́въ

ли́къ: а҆ми́нь.

Вхо́дитⸯ дїа́конъ во ст҃ы́й ѻ҆лта́рь, и҆ а҆́бїе начина́етⸯ ли́къ пѣ́ти со сладкопѣ́нїемъ стїхі́рꙋ на вхо́дъ и҆лѝ настоѧ́щїй тропа́рь, є҆го́же пое́мъ въ недѣ́лю и҆ про́чїи пра́здники[1]:

Є҆диноро́дный сн҃е и҆ сло́ве бж҃їй, безⸯсме́ртенъ сы́й и҆ и҆зво́ливый спⷭе́нїѧ на́шегѡ ра́ди воплоти́тисѧ ѿ ст҃ы́ѧ бц҃ы, и҆ приснодѣ́вы мр҃і́м, непрело́жнѡ вочл҃вѣ́чивыйсѧ: распны́йсѧ же хрⷭ҇тѐ бж҃е, сме́ртїю сме́рть попра́вый, є҆ди́нъ сы́нъ ст҃ы́ѧ трⷪ҇цы, спрославла́емый ѻ҆ц҃ꙋ и҆ ст҃о́мꙋ дх҃ꙋ, спⷭѝ на́съ.

---

[1]Если тропарь **Единородный Сыне** не поется, поемъ тропарь или стихиру праздника изъ Минеи, Трїоди Постной или Цвѣтной.

us to Thy goodness, for Thou art blessed, and to Thee is due glory, to the Father, and to the Son, and to the Holy Spirit, now and ever, and unto the ages of ages.

SINGERS: Amen.

The deacon enters the sanctuary through the lesser door, and immediately, the singers begin to sing the Sticheron for the Entrance[1] or this Troparion, used on Sundays and other solemn days:

Only-begotten Son and Word of God, who art immortal, yet didst deign for our salvation to become incarnate of the holy Theotokos and Ever-Virgin Mary, and without change didst become man, and wast crucified, O Christ our God, trampling down death by death, Thou who art One of the Holy Trinity, glorified together with the Father and the Holy Spirit, save us.

[1]If Only-begotten Son is not sung, we sing the troparion or the sticheron for the Feast from Menaion, Triodion, or Pentecostarion.

Пѣва́емꙋ семꙋ̀ тропарю̀, сщ҃е́нникъ и҆
дїа́конъ прихо́дѧтъ ко ст҃ѣ́й трапе́зѣ и҆
поклонѧ́ютсѧ три́жды. Прїе́мъ сщ҃е́нникъ
ст҃о́е є҆ѵⷢлїе, дае́тъ дїа́конꙋ и҆ и҆дꙋ́тъ чрезъ
сѣ́верныѧ две́ри, предидꙋ́щымъ и҆мъ
кади́льницѣ и҆ лампа́дамъ, и҆ творѧ́тъ
ма́лый вхо́дъ. Прише́дше ко а҆налогі́ю, и҆́же
є҆́сть посредѣ̀ хра́ма, полага́етъ дїа́конъ
ст҃о́е є҆ѵⷢлїе на а҆налогі́й.

И҆дꙋ́тъ всѝ да́же до степе́ней сѡле́й,
и҆ здѣ̀ ста́нꙋтъ, до́ндеже скончаю́тъ
пѣвцы̀ тропа́рь. и҆ ре́кшꙋ дїа́конꙋ:

Го́споди, бл҃гословѝ. Прости,
гл҃етъ сщ҃е́нникъ мл҃твꙋ сїю̀:

Мл҃тва ю҆́же гл҃етъ і҆ере́й на вхо́дъ.

Бж҃е вседержи́телю, великоимени́те гд҃и,
да́вый на́мъ вхо́дъ во ст҃а́ѧ ст҃ы́хъ
прише́ствїемъ є҆диноро́днагѡ твоегѡ̀ сн҃а,
гд҃а же и҆ бг҃а и҆ сп҃са на́шегѡ і҆и҃са хр҃та̀:
про́симъ и҆ мо́лимъ твою̀ бл҃гостыню,
понеже стра́хомъ содержи́ми є҆смы̀ и҆

When the singers begin the Troparion,
the priest and the deacon approach the
holy table and bow three times. The priest
gives the Gospel to the deacon, and they
proceed through the north door, preceded
by the censer-bearers and candle-bearers,
and they make the small entrance.
When they arrive at the analogion in the
middle of the nave, the deacon places the
holy Gospel on the analogion.

They go further to the steps of the solea, and
stand there until the singers finish
the Troparion. After the deacon says,
Lord, bless. Stand upright, the priest
says this prayer:

The prayer that the priest says at the entrance

O God almighty, Lord of the great Name,
who hast given us entrance into the
holy of holies through the coming of Thine
only-begotten Son, our Lord, God, and Saviour Jesus Christ; we entreat and supplicate

тре́петни, хотѧ́ще предста́ти сто́мꙋ
твоемꙋ̀ же́ртвеннику, послѝ на ны̀ бл҃года́ть
твою̀ бл҃гꙋ́ю, и҆ ѡ҆ст҃и́ на́ша дꙋ́ши и҆ тѣлеса̀
и҆ дꙋ́си, и҆ и҆зменѝ мꙋдрова́нїѧ на́ша ко
бл҃гоче́стїю, ꙗ҆́кѡ да въ чи́стѣй со́вѣсти
принесе́мъ тебѣ̀ да́ры, даѧ́нїѧ, плоды̀, во
ѿмета́нїе на́шихъ грѣхѡ́въ и҆ во ѡ҆чище́нїе
всѣ́мъ лю́демъ твои́мъ, бл҃года́тїю и҆
ще́дротами и҆ чл҃вѣколю́бїемъ є҆диноро́днагѡ
сн҃а твоегѡ̀, съ ни́мже бл҃гослове́нъ є҆сѝ, и҆
со прест҃ы́мъ и҆ бл҃ги́мъ и҆ животворѧ́щимъ
твои́мъ дх҃омъ, нн҃ѣ и҆ при́снѡ и҆ во вѣ́ки
вѣкѡ́въ.

Ли́къ: а҆ми́нь.

И҆ вхо́дитъ сщ҃е́нникъ во ст҃и́лище, и҆
ста́нетъ пред ст҃о́ю трапе́зою. Дїа́конъ же
ста́нетъ на ѡ҆бы́чнѣмъ мѣ́стѣ, и҆ гл҃етъ,
зрѧ̀ къ восто́кꙋ, дїа́конства сїѧ̑:

Ми́ромъ гдꙋ помо́лимсѧ.

Ли́къ: Гд҃и, поми́лꙋй.

Thy goodness: as we are about to stand before Thy holy altar, filled with fear and trembling, send upon us Thy good grace, and sanctify our souls, bodies, and spirits, and turn our minds toward piety, so that with a pure conscience we may offer Thee gifts, presents, and fruits for the abolishing of our transgressions and for the propitiation of all Thy people, through the grace and compassions and love for mankind of Thine only-begotten Son, with whom Thou art blessed, together with Thine All-holy, good, and life-giving Spirit, now and ever and unto the ages of ages.

SINGERS: Amen.

The priest enters the sanctuary, and stands before the holy table. Meanwhile, the deacon stands at his usual place outside of the holy doors, and says this litany, facing east:

In peace let us pray to the Lord.
SINGERS: Lord have mercy.

Ѡ҆ свы́шнемъ ми́рѣ и҆ бж҃їемъ чл҃вѣколю́бїи, и҆ спасе́нїи дꙋ́шъ на́шихъ, гдꙋ помо́лимсѧ.

Ли́къ: Гд҃и, поми́лꙋй.

Ѡ҆ ми́рѣ всегѡ̀ мі́ра и҆ соедине́нїи всѣ́хъ ст҃ы́хъ бж҃їихъ цр҃кве́й, гдꙋ помо́лимсѧ.

Ли́къ: Гд҃и, поми́лꙋй.

Ѡ҆ спасе́нїи и҆ застꙋпле́нїи ст҃а́гѡ ѻ҆тца̀ на́шегѡ, а҆рхїепⷭ҇копа (и҆лѝ митрополі́та) и҆м҃къ, ѡ҆ все́мъ при́чтѣ и҆ хрⷭ҇толюби́выхъ лю́дехъ, гдꙋ помо́лимсѧ.

Ли́къ: Гд҃и, поми́лꙋй.

Ѡ҆ бг҃охрани́мѣй странѣ̀ се́й, власте́хъ и҆ во́инствѣ є҆ѧ̀, гдꙋ помо́лимсѧ.

Ли́къ: Гд҃и, поми́лꙋй.

Ѡ҆ ст҃ѣ́мъ гра́дѣ бг҃а на́шегѡ, ѡ҆ цр҃твꙋющемъ гра́дѣ, ѡ҆ гра́дѣ се́мъ (и҆лѝ ѡ҆ ве́си се́й, и҆лѝ ѡ҆ ст҃ѣ́й ѡ҆би́тели се́й) и҆ ѡ҆ всѧ́комъ гра́дѣ и҆ странѣ̀, и҆ ѡ҆ и҆́хже правосла́вною вѣ́рою и҆ бл҃гоче́стїемъ живꙋ́щихъ въ ни́хъ, ѡ҆ ми́рѣ и҆ сохране́нїи и҆́хъ, гдꙋ помо́лимсѧ.

For the peace from above and the love of God for mankind, and the salvation of our souls, let us pray to the Lord.

SINGERS: Lord have mercy.

For the peace of the whole world and the union of all the holy churches of God, let us pray to the Lord.

SINGERS: Lord have mercy.

For the salvation and protection of our holy father, Archbishop [or Metropolitan] N., for all the clergy and Christ-loving people, let us pray to the Lord.

SINGERS: Lord have mercy.

For this God-preserved land, its authorities and armed forces, let us pray to the Lord.

SINGERS: Lord have mercy.

For the holy city of our God, for the royal city, for this city [or: village, or: holy monastery] and for every city and countryside, and for those who in Orthodox faith and piety dwell in them, for their peace and safety, let us pray to the Lord.

Ли́къ: Гдⷭ҇и, поми́лꙋй.

Ѡ҆ ѡ҆ставле́нїи грѣхѡ́въ, и҆ проще́нїи согрѣше́нїй на́шихъ, и҆ ѡ҆ є҆́же и҆зба́витисѧ на́мъ ѿ всѧ́кїѧ ско́рби, гнѣ́ва, нꙋ́жды, и҆ возста́нїѧ ꙗ҆зы́кѡвъ, гдⷭ҇ꙋ помо́лимсѧ.

Ли́къ: Гдⷭ҇и, поми́лꙋй.

Прест҃ꙋ́ю и҆ пребл҃гослове́ннꙋю, пречⷭ҇тꙋ́ю влⷣцꙋ на́шꙋ бцⷣꙋ и҆ приснодв҃ꙋ мр҃і́ю, чⷭ҇тны́ѧ безпло́тныѧ а҆рха́гг҃елы, ст҃а́го і҆ѡа́нна прⷪ҇ро́ка, прⷣте́чꙋ и҆ крⷭ҇ти́телѧ, бж҃е́ственныѧ, сщ҃е́нныѧ сла́вныѧ а҆пⷭ҇лы, прⷪ҇ро́ки и҆ добро_побѣ́дныѧ мч҃ники, и҆ всѧ̀ ст҃ы́ѧ и҆ пра́ведныѧ помѧне́мъ, ꙗ҆́кѡ да мл҃твами и҆ предста́тельствы и҆́хъ всѝ поми́ловани бꙋ́демъ.

Ли́къ: Гдⷭ҇и, поми́лꙋй.

Всѝ предстоѧ́щїѧ, ѡ҆ себѣ̀ самѣ́хъ и҆ дрꙋ́гъ ѡ҆ дрꙋ́зѣ гдⷭ҇ꙋ бг҃ꙋ на́шемꙋ помо́лимсѧ.

Ли́къ: Гдⷭ҇и, поми́лꙋй (г҃_жды).

Сщ҃е́нникъ гл҃етъ та́йнѡ
мл҃твꙋ трист҃а́гѡ:

SINGERS: Lord have mercy.

For the remission of our sins and forgiveness of our offenses, and for our deliverance from all tribulation, wrath, and necessity, and the uprising of the nations, let us pray to the Lord.

SINGERS: Lord have mercy.

Let us call to remembrance our most holy and most blessed and pure Lady Theotokos and Ever-Virgin Mary, the honorable bodiless archangels, the Holy Prophet, Forerunner and Baptist John, the divine, sacred, and glorious apostles, prophets, and passion-bearing martyrs and all the saints and righteous ones, so that by their intercessions we all may receive mercy.

SINGERS: Lord have mercy.

All ye here present, for ourselves and for one another, let us pray to the Lord our God.

SINGERS: Lord have mercy (thrice).

The priest says secretly the
Prayer of the Trisagion:

Ще́дре и҆ ми́лостиве гд҃и, долготер_
пѣли́ве и҆ многоми́лостиве и҆ и҆́стинне,
при́зри ѿ гото́вагѡ жили́ца твоегѡ̀, и҆
оу҆слы́ши ны твои́хъ рабѡ́въ, и҆ и҆зба́ви
на́съ ѿ всѧ́кїѧ напа́сти дїа́вольскїѧ же
и҆ чл҃вѣ́ческїѧ, и҆ не ѿ и҆ми́ ѿ на́съ твою̀
по́мощь, ниже́ тѧжча́йшее па́че на́шеѧ
си́лы наказа́нїе наведе́ши на ны̀. мы̀ бо не
дово́льни е҆смы̀ побѣжда́ти сопроти́вныхъ
находѧ́щихъ, ты̀ же си́ленъ сы́й во е҆́же
спаса́ти ѿ всѣ́хъ сопротивѧ́щихсѧ на́мъ.
спасѝ на́съ гд҃и бж҃е на́шъ ѿ ѕлы́хъ мі́ра
сегѡ̀ по бл҃гости твое́й, ꙗ҆́кѡ да вше́дше
съ чи́стою со́вѣстїю во ст҃ы́й тво́й
же́ртвенникъ, бл҃же́ннꙋю и҆ трист҃ꙋ́ю пѣ́снь съ
небе́сными си́лами неѡсꙋжде́ннѡ возсле́мъ
ти, и҆ бж҃е́ственнꙋю и҆ бл҃гопрїѧ́тнꙋю тебѣ̀
соверши́вше слꙋ́жбꙋ, сподо́бимсѧ жи́зни
вѣ́чныѧ.

Возглаше́нїе:

Ꙗ҆́кѡ ст҃ъ е҆сѝ, гд҃и бж҃е на́шъ, и҆ во ст҃ы́хъ
живе́ши и҆ почива́еши, и҆ тебѣ̀ сла́вꙋ и҆

Ocompassionate and merciful Lord, long-suffering and plenteous in mercy and true: look down from Thy prepared dwelling-place and hear us who entreat Thee, and deliver us from every temptation of the devil and of man, and remove not Thy help from us, neither bring upon us the chastisement that is heavier than we can bear. For we are not able to overcome the things that come upon us, but Thou, O Lord, hast power to save us from all adversities. Save us, O God, from the evils of this world according to Thy goodness, that we, entering with a pure conscience into Thy holy altar, may, together with the heavenly hosts, send up without condemnation the blessed and thrice-holy hymn unto Thee, and completing the divine liturgy which is well-pleasing unto Thee, may be counted worthy of life everlasting.

Exclamation:

For holy art Thou, O Lord our God, and Thou dwellest and restest in the holy place, and unto

трист҃ꙋ́ю пѣ́снь возсыла́емъ, ѻ҆ц҃ꙋ, и҆ сн҃ꙋ, и҆ ст҃о́мꙋ дх҃ꙋ, нн҃ѣ и҆ при́снѡ и҆ во вѣ́ки вѣкѡ́въ.

Ли́къ: а҆ми́нь.

И҆ а҆́бїе пою́тъ пѣвцы̀ трист҃о́е ѻ҆бы́чнѡ:

Ст҃ы́й бж҃е, ст҃ы́й крѣ́пкїй, ст҃ы́й без_ сме́ртный, поми́лꙋй на́съ. (г҃_жды)

Сла́ва: и҆ нн҃ѣ.

Ст҃ы́й безсме́ртный, поми́лꙋй на́съ.

Дїа́конъ: Дѵнамїсъ.

И҆ пою́тъ пѣвцы̀ высоча́йшымъ гла́сомъ:

Ст҃ы́й бж҃е, ст҃ы́й крѣ́пкїй, ст҃ы́й без_ сме́ртный, поми́лꙋй на́съ.

Пѣва́емꙋ же трист҃о́мꙋ, ѿхо́дятъ сщ҃е́нникъ со дїа́кономъ къ го́рнемꙋ мѣ́стꙋ. А҆́ще слꙋ́житъ пресвѵ́теръ, на го́рнее мѣ́сто не восхо́дитъ, но сѣ́дитъ на сопресто́лїи съ сослꙋжа́щими

Thee do we send up glory and the thrice-holy hymn, to the Father ,and to the Son, and to the Holy Spirit, now and ever, and unto the ages of ages.

SINGERS: Amen.

> And immediately, the singers chant
> the Trisagion as usual:

Holy God, Holy Mighty, Holy Immortal, have mercy on us (thrice).

Glory . . . Both now . . .

Holy Immortal, have mercy on us.

DEACON: Dynamis! (Or: With strength!)

> The singers chant in a louder voice:

Holy God, Holy Mighty, Holy Immortal, have mercy on us!

> During the Trisagion hymn, the priest with the deacon proceed to the high place. If a priest celebrates, he does not ascend to the throne, but sits on the synthronon, with the other concelebrating presbyters. If a bishop

пресвѵ́терами. А҆́ще слꙋ́житъ а҆рхїере́й,
то на го́рнее мѣ́сто восхо́дитъ и҆
снима́етъ ѡ҆мофѡ́рїй.

По и҆сполне́нїи трист҃а́гѡ, сщ҃е́нникъ
возглаша́етъ:

Ми́ръ всѣ҄мъ.

И҆ чте́цъ глаго́летъ: И҆ дꙋ́хови твоемꙋ́.

Дїа́конъ: Премꙋ́дрость.

И҆ гл҃етъ чте́цъ: Ѱало́мъ дв҃довъ, гла́съ...,
ꙗ҆́кѡже предписа́са во а҆по́столѣ, и҆
ѿвѣща́ютъ пѣвцы̀ по ѡ҆бы́чаю.

Дїа́конъ: Премꙋ́дрость.

И҆ глаго́летъ чте́цъ надписа́нїе прⷪ҇ро́чества,
а҆́ще чте́тса въ се́й слꙋ́жбѣ.[2]

[2]Согласно преданію древней Іерусалимской
Церкви, въ особыя дни полагались пророческія
чтенія изъ Ветхаго Завѣта. Напримѣръ, согласно
Іерусалимскому лекціонарію, на память св.
царя Давида и св. апостола Іакова 26 декабря
(нынѣ празднуемыхъ въ Недѣлю по Рождествѣ
Христовомъ) можно читать пророчество изъ
Второй книги Царствъ (5, 1-10). На память апостола,
можно читать изъ книги Премудрости Соломона (3,
1-8), а на память святителя, пророчество изъ книги
Притчей (10, 20-25) или Исайи (61, 6-10).

serves, he ascends the throne and removes his omophorion.

After the Trisagion is completed, the Priest exclaims:

Peace be unto all.

READER: And to thy spirit.

DEACON: Wisdom!

The Reader says: The Psalm of David, in tone . . . , as prescribed for the prokeimenon in the Apostolos, with the singers responding.

DEACON: Wisdom!

The Reader says the inscription of the Prophecy (Old Testament reading), if it is read at this service.[2]

---

[2] According to the traditions of the ancient Jerusalem Church, on some special days the prophetic readings from the Old Testament were appointed. For example, according to the Jerusalem Lectionary, for the memory of St David and St James on December 26 (appointed today for the Sunday after Nativity), one may read 2 Samuel 5:1–10. For the commemoration of an Apostle, one could read Wisdom of Solomon 3:1–8, and for the commemoration of a Hierarch, one may read Proverbs 10:20–25 or Isaiah 61:6–10.

Дїа́конъ: Во́нмемъ ст҃о́мꙋ чте́нїю.

Скончавшꙋ́сѧ про́чествꙋ,
гл҃етъ дїа́конъ:

Премꙋ́дрость.

И҆ гл҃етъ чте́цъ надписа́нїе
а҆по́стола.

Дїа́конъ: Во́нмемъ ст҃о́мꙋ чте́нїю.

А҆по́столꙋ же чтꙋ́мꙋ, дїа́конъ, прїе́мъ
кади́льницꙋ и҆ ѳѷмїа́мъ, прихо́дитъ
ко а҆рхїере́ю и҆ли сщ҃е́ннику, и҆ влага́етъ
сщ҃е́нникъ ѳѷмїа́мъ въ кади́льницꙋ, и҆
бл҃гослови́тъ є҆̀, гл҃юще мл҃твꙋ сїю та́йнѡ:

Мл҃тва кади́ла пре́жде є҆ѵⷢ҇лі́а.

Т҇ебѣ̀, и҆спо́лненномꙋ всѧ́кагѡ бл҃гоꙋха́нїѧ
и҆ весе́лїѧ, гдⷭ҇и бж҃е на́шъ, и҆̀хже да́лъ
є҆сѝ на́мъ, прино́симъ кади́ло сїѐ: и҆́же ꙋ҆́бо,
мо́лимсѧ пре́дъ тобо́ю, да вознесе́тсѧ
ѿ смире́нныхъ рꙋ́къ на́шихъ во ст҃ы́й и҆
пренебе́сный тво́й же́ртвенникъ, въ воню̀

DEACON: Let us attend to the holy reading.

> After the Prophecy is complete,
> the Deacon says:

Wisdom!

> The Reader says the inscription of
> the Epistle reading.

DEACON: Let us attend to the holy reading.

> When the Epistle is read, the deacon
> approaches the bishop or the priest with
> the incense and the censer. The priest places
> the incense in the censer, and blesses the
> incense, saying this prayer silently:

Prayer of the Incense before the Gospel

To Thee, O Lord our God, who art filled with every fragrance and gladness, which Thou hast also granted unto us, we offer this incense; we pray unto Thee: may it ascend from our poor hands to Thy holy altar above the heavens, as an odor of good fragrance, for

бл҃гоꙋха́нїѧ, во ѡ҆ставле́нїе согрѣше́нїй
на́шихъ, и҆ во ѡ҆чище́нїе люде́й твои́хъ,
бл҃года́тїю и҆ ще́дротами и҆ чл҃вѣколю́бїемъ
є҆диноро́днагѡ сн҃а твоегѡ̀, съ ни́мже
бл҃гослове́нъ є҆сѝ, и҆ со прест҃ы́мъ и҆ бл҃ги́мъ
и҆ животворѧ́щимъ твои́мъ дх҃омъ, нн҃ѣ
и҆ при́снѡ и҆ во вѣ́ки вѣкѡ́въ, а҆ми́нь.

Сконча́вшꙋсѧ же а҆пⷭлꙋ,
глаго́летъ дїа́конъ:

Премꙋ́дрость.

Чте́цъ гл҃етъ: а҆ллилꙋ́їа, ѱало́мъ дв҃довъ,
гла́съ... съ оу҆ка́занными стїхѝ.

Дїа́конъ же ка́дитъ ст҃ꙋ́ю трапе́зꙋ
ѡ҆́крестъ, и҆ ѻ҆лта́рь, и҆ сщ҃е́нника.
И҆ посе́мъ ѿлага́етъ кади́ло.

Пое́мꙋ же а҆ллилꙋ́їа, сщ҃е́нникъ
глаго́летъ мл҃твꙋ сїю̀ та́йнѡ:

Мл҃тва пре́жде є҆ѵⷢлїа.

Возсїѧ́й въ сердца́хъ на́шихъ. чл҃вѣколю́бче
вл҃ко, твоегѡ̀ бг҃оразꙋ́мїѧ нетлѣ́нный

the remission of our sins and as the propitiation of all thy people. Through the grace and compassions and love for mankind of Thine only-begotten Son, with whom Thou art blessed, together with Thine All-holy, good, and life-giving Spirit, now and ever and unto ages of ages. Amen.

When the Epistle is complete,
the deacon says:

Wisdom!

The Reader says: **Alleluia, the Psalm of David, in . . . tone,** with the appointed verses.

The deacon censes the holy table,
the sanctuary, and the priest.
Then he gives away the censer.

While the Alleluia is intoned,
the priest reads this prayer quietly:

Prayer before the Gospel

Shine forth within our hearts the incorruptible light of Thy knowledge, O Mas-

све́тъ, и҆ мы́сленныѧ на́ши ѿве́рзи ѻ҆́чи, во
є҆ѵⷢльскихъ твои́хъ проповѣ́данїй разꙋмѣ́нїе:
вложи́ въ на́съ и҆ стра́хъ бл҃же́нныхъ твои́хъ
за́повѣдей, да плотскі́ѧ по́хѡти всѧ̂
попра́вше, дꙋхо́вное жи́тельство про́йдемъ,
всѧ̂, ꙗ҆́же ко бл҃гоꙋгожде́нїю твоемꙋ̀, и҆
мꙋ́дрствꙋюще и҆ дѣ́юще.

Ты́ бо є҆сѝ бл҃говѣ́стїе и҆ просвѣще́нїе,
сп҃съ и҆ храни́тель дꙋ́шъ и҆ тѣле́съ на́шихъ,
бж҃е, и҆ є҆диноро́дный тво́й сн҃ъ, и҆ дх҃ъ
тво́й прест҃ы́й, ны́нѣ и҆ при́снѡ и҆ во вѣ́ки
вѣкѡ́въ, а҆ми́нь.

Посе́мъ и҆схо́дитъ дїа́конъ ст҃ыми
две́рми на а҆мвѡ́нъ посредѣ̀ цр҃кве, гдѣ̀
полага́етсѧ ст҃о́е є҆ѵⷢлїе. Ста́ѧ на а҆мвѡ́нѣ,
дїа́конъ возглаша́етъ:

Про́сти, ѹ҆слы́шимъ ст҃а́гѡ є҆ѵⷢлїа.

Сщ҃е́нникъ: Ми́ръ всѣ́мъ.
Ли́къ: И҆ дꙋ́хови твоемꙋ̀.
Дїа́конъ: Ѿ и҆́мⷦъ ст҃а́гѡ є҆ѵⷢлїа чте́нїе.

ter who lovest mankind, and open the eyes of our mind to the understanding of the preaching of Thy Gospel. Instill in us also the fear of Thy blessed commandments, that trampling down all lusts of the flesh, we may pursue a spiritual way of life, both thinking and doing what is well-pleasing unto Thee.

For Thou art the good tidings and illumination, the Saviour and guardian of our souls and bodies, O God, Thou and Thine Only-begotten Son, and Thine All-holy Spirit, now and ever and unto the ages of ages. Amen.

Then, the deacon proceeds through the holy doors to the ambo in the middle of the church where the Gospel is placed. When on the ambo, the deacon exclaims:

Aright! Let us hear the holy Gospel.

PRIEST: Peace be unto all.
SINGERS: And to thy spirit.
DEACON: The reading is from the holy Gospel according to N.

Ли́къ: Сла́ва тебѣ̀, гдⷭ҇и, сла́ва тебѣ̀.

Вторы́й дїа́конъ и҆лѝ сщ҃е́нникъ:
Во́нмемъ ст҃о́мꙋ чте́нїю.

Сконча́вшꙋсѧ же є҆ѵⷢ҇льскомꙋ чте́нїю,
ли́къ пое́тъ: Сла́ва тебѣ̀, гдⷭ҇и, сла́ва тебѣ̀,
и҆ наставлѧ́етъ сщ҃е́нникъ лю́ди
въ сло́вѣ бж҃їемъ.

Посе́мъ ста́нетъ дїа́конъ на ѡ҆бы́чнѣмъ
мѣ́стѣ, зрѧ̀ къ восто́кꙋ, и҆ глаго́летъ
дїа́конства сїѧ̀:

Рце́мъ всѝ: гдⷭ҇и поми́лꙋй.

Ли́къ: Гдⷭ҇и поми́лꙋй.

Гдⷭ҇и вседержи́телю, небе́сне бж҃е ѻ҆те́цъ
на́шихъ, мо́лимъ ти сѧ, ѹ҆слы́ши и҆
поми́лꙋй.

Ли́къ: Гдⷭ҇и поми́лꙋй.

Ѡ҆ ми́рѣ всегѡ̀ мі́ра и҆ соедине́нїи всѣ́хъ
ст҃ы́хъ бж҃їихъ цр҃кве́й, мо́лимъ ти сѧ,
ѹ҆слы́ши и҆ поми́лꙋй.

Ли́къ: Гдⷭ҇и поми́лꙋй.

Ѡ҆ спасе́нїи и҆ застꙋпле́нїи ст҃а́гѡ ѻ҆ц҃а̀

SINGERS: Glory to Thee, O Lord, glory to Thee.

Second deacon or priest:
Let us attend to the holy reading.

After the Gospel reading is complete,
the singers chant: Glory to Thee, O Lord,
glory to Thee, and the Priest instructs
the people in the word of God.

Then the deacon stands in the usual place,
facing east, and says this litany:

Let us all say: Lord have mercy.

SINGERS: Lord have mercy.

O Lord almighty, heavenly God of our fathers, we pray Thee, hearken and have mercy.

SINGERS: Lord have mercy.

For the peace of the whole world and for the union of all the holy churches of God, we pray Thee, Lord, hearken and have mercy.

SINGERS: Lord have mercy.

For the salvation and protection of our holy father, Archbishop [or Metropolitan] N.,

на́шегѡ, а҆рхїепⷭкопа (и҆лѝ митрополі́та)
и҆мⷬкъ, ѡ҆ все́мъ при́чтѣ и҆ хрⷭтолюби́выхъ
лю́дехъ, мо́лимъ ти сѧ, ѹ҆слы́ши и҆
поми́луй.

Ли́къ: Гдⷭи, поми́луй.

Ѡ҆ бг҃охрани́мѣй странѣ̀ се́й, власте́хъ и҆
во́инствѣ є҆ѧ̀, мо́лимъ ти сѧ, ѹ҆слы́ши и҆
поми́луй.

Ли́къ: Гдⷭи, поми́луй.

И҆ ѡ҆ предстоѧ́щихъ лю́дехъ, ѡ҆жида́-
ющихъ ѿ тебє̀, гдⷭи, вели́кїѧ и҆ бога́тыѧ
ми́лости, мо́лимъ тѧ̀, бу́ди бл҃гоѹтро́бенъ,
и҆ поми́луй.

Ли́къ: Гдⷭи, поми́луй.

Спаси́, бж҃е, лю́ди твоѧ̀, и҆ бл҃гословѝ
достоѧ́нїе твоѐ, посѣтѝ мі́ръ тво́й ми́ло-
стїю и҆ щедро́тами, возвы́си ро́гъ хрⷭтїа́нъ
правосла́вныхъ си́лою живоворѧ́щагѡ
крⷭта̀ и҆ мл҃твами престⷭы́ѧ, пречⷭты́ѧ,
пребл҃гослове́нныѧ влⷣцы на́шеѧ бцⷣы и҆
приснодв҃ы мр҃і́и, і҆ѡа́нна прⷣте́чи, а҆пⷭлѡвъ
и҆ всѣ́хъ ст҃ы́хъ твои́хъ, мо́лимъ тѧ̀

of all the clergy and the Christ-loving people, we pray Thee: hearken and have mercy.

SINGERS: Lord have mercy.

For this God-preserved land, its authorities and armed forces, we pray Thee: hearken and have mercy.

SINGERS: Lord have mercy.

And for the people here present who await of Thee, O Lord, great and abundant mercy, we pray Thee: be compassionate and have mercy.

SINGERS: Lord have mercy.

Save, O God, thy people, and bless Thine inheritance, visit thy world with mercy and compassion; exalt the horn of Orthodox Christians by the power of the life-giving Cross and by the intercessions of our most holy, most pure, most blessed Lady Theotokos and Ever-Virgin Mary, of John the Forerunner, of the Apostles and of all Thy saints, we pray Thee, O Lord plenteous in mercy,

многомл҇тиве гд҃и, ѹ҆слы́ши на́съ, грѣ́ш_
ныхъ, моля́щихсѧ тебѣ̀, и҆ поми́лꙋй на́съ.

Ли́къ: Гд҃и, поми́лꙋй, г҃_жды.

Сщ҃е́нникъ глаго́летъ та́йнѡ мл҃твꙋ сїю̀:

Мл҃тва по є҆ѵⷢлїн.

Б Ж҃е, ѡ҆гласи́вый ны̀ бж҃е́ственными
Т твои́ми и҆ спаси́тельными словесы̀,
просвѣтѝ и҆ дꙋ́ши на́съ грѣ́шныхъ во
преждече́нныхъ разꙋмѣ́нїе, ꙗ҆́кѡ не то́чїю
слы́шателемъ на́мъ ꙗ҆ви́тисѧ дх҃о́вныхъ
пѣ́сней, но и҆ творца́мъ дѣѧ́нїй бы́ти, вѣ́рꙋ
проходѧ́ще неле́стнꙋ, житїѐ непоро́чно и҆
жи́знь непови́ннꙋ.

Возглаше́нїе:

Ѡ҆ хрⷭтѣ̀ і҆и҃сѣ гдⷭѣ на́шемъ, съ ни́мже
блгⷭве́нъ є҆сѝ, и҆ со престы́мъ и҆ бл҃ги́мъ
и҆ животворѧ́щимъ твои́мъ дх҃омъ, ны́нѣ
и҆ при́снѡ и҆ во вѣ́ки вѣкѡ́въ.

Ли́къ: А҆ми́нь.

Сщ҃е́нникъ: Ми́ръ всѣ̑мъ.

hearken unto us sinners who pray unto Thee, and have mercy on us.

SINGERS: Lord have mercy (thrice).

The priest says this prayer secretly:

Prayer after the Gospel

O God who hast inspired us with Thy divine and saving oracles, illumine the souls of us sinners for the comprehension of the things that were just read, so that we may be shown not only as hearers of spiritual songs, but also as doers of good works, maintaining a faith without pretense, a life without blame, conduct without reproach.

Exclamation:

In Christ Jesus our Lord, with whom Thou art blessed and glorified, together with Thine All-holy, good, and life-giving Spirit, now and ever and unto the ages of ages.

SINGERS: Amen.

PRIEST: Peace be unto all.

Ли́къ: И҆ дꙋ́хови твоемꙋ̀.

Дїа́конъ: Главы̀ на́ша гдⷭ҇еви приклѻ́нимъ.

Ли́къ: Тебѣ̀, гдⷭ҇и.

Сщⷲе́нникъ мл҃твꙋ
главопреклоне́нїѧ та́йнѡ:

Ꙗ҆́ко животво́рче и҆ бла҃ги́хъ пода́телю, да́вый чл҃вѣ́кѡмъ бл҃же́ннꙋю наде́ждꙋ вѣ́чныѧ жи́зни, гдⷭ҇а на́шего і҆и҃са хрⷭ҇та̀, сподо́би на́съ, бл҃гі́й, во ѡ҆сщⷲе́нїи и҆ сїю̀ ти бжⷭ҇тве́ннꙋю соверши́ти слꙋ́жбꙋ въ наслажде́нїе бꙋ́дꙋщагѡ бл҃же́нства.

Возглаше́нїе:

Ꙗ҆́кѡ да под̾ держа́вою твое́ю всегда̀ храни́ми и҆ во свѣ́тъ и҆́стины пꙋтеводи́ми, тебѣ̀ сла́вꙋ и҆ бл҃годаре́нїе возсыла́емъ, ѻ҆ц҃ꙋ, и҆ сн҃ꙋ, и҆ ст҃о́мꙋ дх҃ꙋ, нынѣ и҆ при́снѡ и҆ во вѣ́ки вѣкѡ́въ.

Ли́къ: а҆ми́нь.

И҆ посе́мъ, дїа́конъ:

SINGERS: And to thy spirit.

DEACON: Let us bow our heads unto the Lord.

SINGERS: To Thee, O Lord.

> The priest says quietly this prayer
> of the bowing of the heads:

O Master, the Giver of life and Provider of good things, who gavest to men the blessed hope of eternal life, our Lord Jesus Christ, make us worthy, O Good one, in holiness to complete this divine liturgy to Thee for the delight of the blessedness which is to come.

Exclamation:

That always guarded by Thy might and guided to the light of truth, we may send up glory and thanksgiving unto Thee, to the Father, and to the Son, and to the Holy Spirit, now and ever, and unto the ages of ages.

SINGERS: Amen.

And thereafter, the deacon:

Ми́ромъ хрто́вымъ воспои́мъ.

И҆ пою́тъ пѣвцы̀ стїхи́рꙋ на ᲂу҆мове́нїе рꙋ́къ.[3] А҆́ще слꙋ́житъ а҆рхїере́й, ᲂу҆мыва́етъ рꙋ́ки.

Посе́мъ глаго́летъ дїа́конъ:

Да никто̀ ѿ ѡ҆глаше́нныхъ, да никто̀ ѿ непосвꙗще́нныхъ, да никто̀ ѿ немогꙋ́щихъ съ на́ми помоли́тисѧ. Дрꙋ́гъ дрꙋ́га позна́йте, дрꙋ́гъ дрꙋ́га ᲂу҆вѣ́дите. Две́ри затвори́те, про́сти всѝ.

И҆ вхо́дитъ дїа́конъ во стꙑ́й ѻ҆лта́рь, и҆ начина́ютъ пѣвцы̀ ко́снѡ и҆ со сладкопѣ́нїемъ стїхи́рꙋ во стꙑ́лъ, сїю̀:

Да молчи́тъ всꙗ́каꙗ пло́ть чл҃вѣ́ча, и҆ да стои́тъ со стра́хомъ и҆ тре́петомъ, и҆ ничто́же земно́е въ себѣ̀ да помышлꙗ́етъ:

[3] Въ древней Іерусалимской Церкви, стихира на умовеніе рукъ находилась въ составѣ пѣснопѣній древнꙗго Іерусалимскаго Тропологія. Въ отсутствіе полнаго перевода песнопѣній древнꙗго Тропологія, стихира на умовеніе рукъ можетъ быть выбрана изъ числа праздничныхъ стихиръ Минеи, Октоиха, Тріоди Постной или Цвѣтной.

In the peace of Christ, let us sing!

The Singers chant the Sticheron for the Washing of Hands.[3] If the bishop serves, he washes his hands here.

Then, the deacon says:

Let none of the catechumens remain, let none of the uninitiated, let none of those who are unable to pray with us remain! Recognize each other, know each other! Shut the doors! All stand aright!

The deacon enters the sanctuary, and the Singers begin to sing this Sticheron for the Holy Gifts, slowly and with sweet singing:

Let all mortal flesh keep silence, and stand with fear and trembling; and let it take no thought for any earthly thing. For the King of

[3]In the ancient Jerusalem Church, the sticheron for the washing of hands was found among the hymns of the ancient Jerusalem Tropologion. In the absence of the full translation of the hymns of the ancient Tropologion, the sticheron for the washing of hands may be selected from the festal stichera of the Menaion, Octoechos, Triodion or Pentecostarion.

цр҃ь бо цр҃тꙋ́ющихъ и҆ гд҃ь госпо́дствꙋющихъ
прихо́дитъ заклати́сѧ и҆ да́тисѧ въ снѣ́дь
вѣ́рнымъ.

Пѣва́емѣй се́й стїхі́рѣ, прино́ситъ
дїа́конъ кади́льницꙋ съ ѳѷмїа́момъ,
и҆ бл҃гослови́тъ ю҆̀ сщ҃е́нникъ,
гл҃юще мл҃твꙋ сїю̀:

Мл҃тва кади́ла.

Ꙗ҆́ко вседержи́телю, цр҃ю̀ сла́вы, вѣ́дый
всѧ̀ пре́жде сбытїѧ̀ чл҃вѣ́ческа, са́мъ
прїидѝ къ на́мъ въ ча́съ се́й молѧ́щимъ ти́
сѧ, и҆ и҆зба́ви на́съ ѿ стꙋда̀ прегрѣше́нїй,
ѡ҆чи́сти на́шъ ᲂу҆́мъ и҆ помышле́нїѧ ѿ
скве́рныхъ жела́нїй, и҆ сꙋемꙋ́дрїѧ мі́ра
сегѡ̀, и҆ всѧ́кагѡ дїа́вольскагѡ дѣ́йствїѧ,
и҆ прїимѝ ѿ рꙋ́къ на́съ грѣ́шныхъ кади́ло
сїѐ въ воню̀ бл҃гоꙋха́нїѧ, ꙗ҆́коже прїѧ́тъ
приноше́нїе а҆́велево, а҆враа́мово, а҆арѡ́ново,
самꙋ́илово, заха́рїнно, и҆ всѣ́хъ ст҃ы́хъ
твои́хъ, и҆ и҆збавлѧ́ѧ на́съ ѿ всѧ́кїѧ
лꙋка́выѧ ве́щи, и҆ спаса́ѧ во є҆́же всегда̀
ᲂу҆гожда́ти, поклана́тисѧ, и҆ сла́вити тебѣ̀,

kings and Lord of lords draweth nigh to be sacrificed and given as food to the faithful.

As this Sticheron is sung, the deacon brings the censer with incense to the priest who blesses it, saying this prayer:

Prayer of Incense

O Master almighty, King of glory, God who knowest all before they come into being, do Thou Thyself be present with us at this holy hour as we call upon Thee, and deliver us from the shame of transgressions, purify our mind and reasoning from unclean thoughts, worldly deceit, and every action of the devil, and receive from the hands of us sinners this incense for an odor of good fragrance, as Thou didst receive the offering of Abel and Noah, of Aaron and Samuel, and of all Thy saints, setting us free from every evil deed and saving us, so that we may always be well-pleasing before Thee, and may worship Thee and glorify Thee, the Father, and Thine

ѻ҆ц҃а̀, и҆ є҆диноро́днагѡ твоегѡ̀ сн҃а, и҆ всест҃а́гѡ
твоегѡ̀ дх҃а, ны́нѣ и҆ при́снѡ и҆ во вѣ́ки
вѣкѡ́въ, а҆ми́нь.

дїа́конъ же кади́тъ ст҃ꙋ́ю трапе́зꙋ
ѡ҆́крестъ, и҆ ѻ҆лта́рь, и҆ ст҃ы́ѧ і҆кѡ́ны,
ли́ки, и҆ всѧ̀ лю́ди.

сщ҃е́нникъ же, ста́въ пре́дъ ст҃о́ю
трапе́зою, глаго́летъ мл҃твы сїѧ̀:

мл҃тва ст҃а́гѡ васі́лїа вели́кагѡ.

Никто́же досто́инъ ѿ свѧза́вшихсѧ
плотски́ми похотьмѝ и҆ сластьмѝ
приходи́ти, и҆лѝ приближи́тисѧ, и҆лѝ
слꙋжи́ти тебѣ̀, цр҃ю̀ сла́вы: є҆́же бо
слꙋжи́ти тебѣ̀, вели́ко и҆ стра́шно и҆
самѣ́мъ нб҃нымъ си́ламъ. но ѻ҆ба́че
неи҆зрече́ннагѡ ра́ди и҆ безмѣ́рнагѡ твоегѡ̀
человѣколю́бїа, непрело́жнѡ и҆ неи҆змѣ́ннѡ
бы́лъ є҆сѝ чл҃вѣ́къ, и҆ а҆рхїере́й на́мъ бы́лъ
є҆сѝ: и҆ слꙋже́бныѧ сеѧ̀ и҆ безкро́вныѧ
же́ртвы сщ҃еннодѣ́йствїе преда́лъ є҆сѝ на́мъ,
ꙗ҆́кѡ влⷣка всѣ́хъ. ты̀ бо є҆ди́нъ, гдⷵи бж҃е

Only-begotten Son, and Thine All-holy Spirit, now and ever and unto ages of ages. Amen.

And the deacon censes the holy table, the sanctuary, the holy icons, the clergy, the choirs and all the people.

Meanwhile, the priest stands before the holy table, saying these prayers:

Prayer of St Basil the Great

None is worthy among them that are bound with carnal lusts and pleasures to approach or to draw near or to minister unto Thee, O King of glory; for to serve Thee is a great and fearful thing even unto the heavenly hosts themselves. Yet because of Thine ineffable and immeasurable love for mankind, without change or alteration Thou didst become man, and didst become our High Priest, and didst deliver unto us the ministry of this liturgical and bloodless sacrifice, for Thou art the Master of all. For Thou alone, O Lord our God, dost rule over those in heaven and those

на́шъ, вл҃чествꙋеши нбⷭ҇ными и҆ земны́ми,
и҆́же на пⷭ҇то́лѣ херꙋві́мстѣ носи́мый,
и҆́же серафі́мшвъ гдⷭ҇ь, и҆ цр҃ь і҆и҃левъ, и҆́же
є҆ди́нъ ст҃ъ, и҆ во ст҃ы́хъ почива́й. та̀ ᲂу҆́бѡ
молю̀ є҆ди́наго бл҃га́го и҆ бл҃гопослꙋ́шливаго:
при́зри на мѧ̀ грѣ́шнаго и҆ непотре́бнаго
раба̀ твоегѡ̀, и҆ ѡ҆чи́сти мою̀ дꙋ́шꙋ и҆ се́рдце
ѿ со́вѣсти лꙋка́выѧ, и҆ ᲂу҆добли́ мѧ, си́лою
ст҃а́гѡ твоегѡ̀ дх҃а, ѡ҆блече́нна бл҃года́тїю
сщ҃е́нства, предста́ти ст҃ѣ́й твое́й се́й
трапе́зѣ, и҆ сщ҃еннодѣ́йствовати ст҃о́е и҆
пречⷭ҇то́е твоѐ тѣ́ло, и҆ честнꙋ́ю кро́вь. къ
тебѣ̀ бо прихождꙋ̀ приклонь̀ мою̀ вы́ю, и҆
молю̀ ти сѧ, да не ѿврати́ши лица̀ твоегѡ̀
ѿ менѐ, нижѐ ѿри́неши менѐ ѿ ѻ҆́трѡкъ
твои́хъ: но сподо́би принесе́нным тебѣ̀
бы́ти, мно́ю грѣ́шнымъ и҆ недосто́йнымъ
рабо́мъ твои́мъ, дарѡ́мъ си́мъ. ты̀ бо
є҆сѝ приносѧ́й и҆ приноси́мый, и҆ прїе́млѧй
и҆ раздава́емый хрⷭ҇тѐ бж҃е на́шъ, и҆ тебѣ̀
сла́вꙋ возсыла́емъ, со безнача́льнымъ
твои́мъ ѻ҆ц҃е́мъ, и҆ престы́мъ, и҆ благи́мъ,

on earth, art borne upon the throne of the cherubim, art Lord of the seraphim and King of Israel, Thou alone art holy and restest in the saints. I implore Thee, therefore, who alone art good and inclined to listen: look down upon me, Thy sinful and unprofitable servant, and purge my soul and heart of a wicked conscience, and by the power of the Holy Spirit enable me, who am clothed with the grace of the priesthood, to stand before this Thy holy table, and to perform the sacred mystery of Thy holy and immaculate Body and precious Blood. For I draw nigh unto Thee, and bowing my neck I pray Thee: turn not Thy countenance away from me, neither cast me out from among Thy children; but vouchsafe that these gifts be offered unto Thee by me, Thy sinful and unworthy servant. For Thou art He that offers and is offered, that accepts and is distributed, O Christ our God, and unto Thee do we send up glory, together with Thine unoriginate Father, and Thine All-holy, good,

й животворѧ́щимъ твои́мъ дх҃омъ, ны́нѣ
й при́снѡ, й во вѣ́ки вѣкѡ́въ, а҆ми́нь.

Мл҃тва в҃, ст҃а́гѡ дїонѵ́сїа а҆реопагі́та.

Стра́шнагѡ твоегѡ̀, гд҃и, предвари́вше
ѻ҆лтарѧ̀, чꙋди́мсѧ лице́мъ, свѣ́тлѣй ти
трапе́зѣ приходѧ́ще, й бли́зъ стра́шнагѡ
твоегѡ̀ бы́вше ст҃и́лища, притре́петни
є҆смы̀, стра́хомъ оу҆́ды коле́блеми, во є҆́же
непоро́чнꙋю сщ҃е́ннꙋю же́ртвꙋ приноси́ти.
кто̀ бо й҆́же земны́мъ прилеплѧ́йсѧ стра-
сте́мъ, дово́ленъ таковы́мъ та́инствомъ
прикаса́тисѧ мо́жетъ бы́ти; воздыма́етъ
бо дерзнове́нїе є҆стества̀ не́мощь, й
со́вѣсть ѡ҆скверне́нна оу҆́мъ содѣва́етъ,
мра́къ покрыва́етъ дꙋши̑ зрѣ́нїе, нечи́сто
жи́тельство, й житїѐ поро́чно. тѣ́мже при-
падо́хомъ й оу҆жасо́хомсѧ, й коле́блемсѧ,
є҆да̀, ꙗ҆́кѡ недосто́йни, дарѡ́мъ прикаса́емсѧ,
ѡ҆брати́мъ же на себѐ бж҃е́ственное ѿмще́нїе.
тѣ́мже мо́лимсѧ твоемꙋ̀ чл҃вѣколю́бїю:
да́ждь на́мъ безстра́шнѣ ст҃ы́мъ ти та́ин-
ствомъ пристꙋпи́ти й оу҆крѣпѝ на́ши

and life-giving Spirit, now and ever and unto the ages of ages. Amen.

Second Prayer,
of St Dionysius the Areopagite:

As we attain to Thy fearful place, O Lord, our faces are utterly amazed when we approach Thy radiant table, and, drawing near to Thy fearsome sanctuary, we are distressed and our members quiver and shake as we bring forth the unapproachable sacred Victim. For who among those on earth, bound to the passions, has power to grasp worthily such mysteries? The weakness of our nature drives away our boldness, and our wretched conscience prevails over the mind, and darkness sets on the eye of our soul, a dishonorable living and a blemished life! Hence we are full of dread and are distressed with fear, lest as we unworthily touch the gifts, we bring upon ourselves Divine judgment. Therefore we entreat Thy love for mankind: grant us to approach Thy Holy Mysteries without fear, and strengthen

дꙋши́ и҆ тѣлеса̀, и҆ да́ждь на́мъ непоро́чнѡ
сщ҃е́нствовати твое́й неи҆зрече́нней си́лѣ.
всѧ̑ бо тобо́ю въ бытїѐ прихо́дѧтъ, и҆
тебѣ̀ подоба́етъ всѧ́каѧ сла́ва, че́сть и҆
великолѣ́пїе, ѻ҆ц҃ꙋ̀, и҆ сн҃ꙋ, и҆ ст҃о́мꙋ дх҃ꙋ,
ны́нѣ и҆ при́снѡ и҆ во вѣ́ки вѣкѡ́въ, а҆ми́нь.

И҆спо́лньшымсѧ же мл҃твамъ и҆ кажде́нїю,
сщ҃е́нникъ и҆ дїа́конъ поклана́ютсѧ
ст҃о́й трапе́зѣ три́жды и҆ ѿхо́дѧтъ въ
предложе́нїе. и҆ оу҆мыва́етъ рꙋ́ки сщ҃е́нникъ
та́мѡ. Посе́мъ подае́тъ дїа́конꙋ ст҃ы́й
ді́скосъ, гл҃юще ѻ҆бы́чныѧ мл҃твы.
Сщ҃е́нникъ ст҃ы́й потꙋ́ръ въ рꙋ́цѣ
прїе́млетъ, и҆ и҆схо́дѧтъ сѣ́верною страно́ю,
предходѧ́щымъ и҆̀мъ лампа́дамъ, рꙗпі́дамъ
и҆ кади́льницамъ. И҆ достѝгше а҆мвѡ́на,
и҆́же є҆́сть посредѣ̀ хра́ма, ста́нꙋтъ
сщ҃е́нникъ со дїа́кономъ на степе́ни є҆гѡ̀,
зрѧ́ще къ за́падꙋ, и҆ гл҃етъ сщ҃е́нникъ:

Всѣ́хъ ва́съ правосла́вныхъ хрⷭ҇тїа́нъ да
помѧне́тъ гдⷭ҇ь бг҃ъ во црⷭ҇твїи свое́мъ всегда̀,
ны́нѣ и҆ при́снѡ и҆ во вѣ́ки векѡ́въ.

our souls and bodies, and grant that we may celebrate this liturgy by Thine inexpressible power, for all things come into being through Thee, and unto Thee is due all glory, honor, and magnificence, to the Father, and to the Son, and to the Holy Spirit, now and ever and unto ages of ages. Amen.

When the censing and the prayers are complete, the priest and the deacon venerate the holy table three times and proceed to the prothesis. The priest washes his hands there. Then he gives the deacon the holy diskos, with the usual words. The priest takes the holy chalice, and they make the entrance, preceded by the candle-bearers, fan-bearers, and censer-bearers. Upon reaching the ambo, the priest and the deacon stand on the steps of the ambo, looking to the west, and the priest says:

All of you Orthodox Christians, may the Lord God remember in His kingdom, always, now and ever and unto ages of ages.

ли́къ, ко́снѡ: а҆ми́нь.

И҆ вни́дꙋтъ сщ7е́нникъ со дїа́кономъ
во ст7ы́й ѻ҆лта́рь и҆ поставлѧ́ютъ ст7ы́ѧ
да́ры на ст7о́й трапе́зѣ, и҆ взима́етъ
сщ7е́нникъ покрѡ́вцы ѿ ст7а́гѡ ді́скоса и҆
ст7а́гѡ потира. возд@хъ же ѿ дїа́кона
ра́ма взе́мъ, покади́въ, покрыва́етъ
и҆́мъ да́ры. кадѧ́ще же сїа̀, гл7етъ
возгла́снѡ мл7твꙋ сїю̀:

Мл7тва предложе́нїѧ.

Бж7е, бж7е на́шъ, небе́сный хлѣ́бъ, пищꙋ
всемꙋ̀ мі́рꙋ, гдⷭа на́шегѡ и҆ бг7а і҆и7са хрⷭта̀
посла́вый сп7са, и҆ и҆зба́вителѧ и҆ бл7годѣ́телѧ,
бл7гословѧ́ща и҆ ѡ҆сщ7а́юща на́съ, са́мъ
бл7гослови́ предложе́нїе сїѐ, и҆ прїими́ є҆̀ въ
пренебе́сный тво́й же́ртвенникъ. помѧни́,
ꙗ҆́кѡ бл7гъ и҆ чл7вѣколю́бецъ, прине́сшихъ, и҆
и҆́хже ра́ди принесо́ша: и҆ на́съ неѡсꙋжде́ны
сохрани́ во сщ7еннодѣ́йствїи бж7е́ственныхъ
твои́хъ та́инъ.

Ꙗ҆́кѡ ст7и́сѧ и҆ просла́висѧ пречⷭтно́е,

SINGERS, SLOWLY: **Amen.**

Then the priest and the deacon enter
the sanctuary and deposit the holy gifts
upon the holy table and the priest removes
the veils from the diskos and the chalice.
He takes the aer from the deacon's shoulder,
covers the holy things with it, censes
the gifts, and says this prayer aloud:

Prayer of the Offering

O God, our God, who didst send forth
the heavenly Bread, the food of the
whole world, our Lord and God, Jesus Christ,
the Saviour, Redeemer, and Benefactor who
blesseth and sanctifieth us: do Thou Thyself
bless this offering, and accept it upon Thine
altar above the heavens. Remember those
who offered it and those for whom it was offered, for Thou art good and lovest mankind,
and preserve us blameless in the sacred celebration of Thy divine mysteries.

For sanctified and glorified is Thine all-

и҆ великолѣ́пое и҆́мѧ твоѐ, Ѻ҆ц҃а̀, и҆ сн҃а, и҆ ст҃а́гѡ дх҃а, ны́нѣ и҆ при́снѡ, и҆ во вѣ́ки вѣкѡ́въ.

Ли́къ: а҆ми́нь.

И҆ па́ки пою́тъ пѣ́вцы̀ стїхі́рꙋ во ст҃а́:

Предхо́дѧтъ же семꙋ̀ ли́цы а҆́гг҃ельстїи со всѧ́кимъ нача́ломъ и҆ вла́стїю, многоѻ́читїи херꙋві́ми, и҆ шестокрила́тїи серафи́ми, ли́ца закрыва́юще, и҆ вопїю́ще пѣ́снь: а҆ллилꙋ́їа (г҃-жды).

Дїа́конъ, прїе́мъ бл҃гослове́нїе, и҆схо́дитъ сѣ́верными две́рми и҆ ста́нетъ на ѻ҆бы́чнѣмъ мѣ́стѣ.

Сконча́вшꙋсѧ же пѣ́нїю, возглаша́етъ дїа́конъ:

Премꙋ́дростїю бж҃їею во́нмемъ.

Сщ҃е́нникъ начина́етъ сѵ́мволъ вѣ́ры, гл҃ѧ: Вѣ́рꙋю во є҆ди́наго бг҃а:

И҆ глаго́лютъ лю́дїе вкꙋ́пѣ: Ѻ҆ц҃а̀ вседержи́телѧ, и҆ па́ки до конца̀.

honorable and majestic name, of the Father,
and of the Son, and of the Holy Spirit, now
and ever, and unto the ages of ages.
SINGERS: Amen.

And the Singers complete the
Sticheron for the holy gifts:
Before Him go the choirs of angels with all
the principalities and powers, the many-eyed
cherubim and the six winged seraphim, cov-
ering their faces and crying aloud the hymn:
Alleluia (thrice).

The deacon receives the blessing,
exits through the north door and
stands in the usual place.

When the hymn is completed,
the deacon exclaims:
In the wisdom of God let us attend!

The priest begins the Creed by saying:
I believe in one God . . .

And the people continue together:
the Father Almighty . . . until the end.

Глаго́лемꙋ же и҆сповѣ́данїю вѣ́ры,
сщ҃éнникъ мо́литсѧ та́йнѡ:

Мл҃тва пре́жде цѣлова́нїѧ.

Всѣ́хъ бж҃е и҆ влⷣко, досто́йны ны содѣ́лай
ст҃а́гѡ часа̀ сегѡ̀, недосто́йныхъ, чл҃вѣко-
лю́бче, ꙗ҆́кѡ да ѡ҆чи́стившесѧ всѧ́кагѡ
лꙋка́вства и҆ ле́сти, соединѝмсѧ дрꙋ́гъ дрꙋ́гꙋ
ми́ра и҆ любвѐ сою́зомъ, оу҆тверждéни твоегѡ̀
бг҃опозна́нїѧ ѡ҆сщ҃éнїемъ, є҆диноро́днагѡ
ра́ди твоегѡ̀ сн҃а, гдⷭ҇а же и҆ сп҃са на́шегѡ
і҆и҃са хрⷭ҇та̀, съ ни́мже блⷭ҇гослове́нъ є҆сѝ, со
прест҃ы́мъ и҆ бл҃ги́мъ и҆ животворѧ́щимъ
твои́мъ дх҃омъ, нн҃ѣ и҆ при́снѡ и҆ во вѣ́ки
вѣкѡ́въ, а҆ми́нь.

И҆спо́лнившꙋсѧ же и҆сповѣ́данїю вѣ́ры,
возглаша́етъ дїа́конъ:
Ста́немъ до́брѣ: ми́ромъ гдⷭ҇ꙋ помо́лимсѧ.

Сщ҃éнникъ, возглаше́нїе:

Ꙗ҆́кѡ бг҃ъ ми́ра, ми́лости, любвѐ, щедро́тъ,
и҆ чл҃вѣколю́бїѧ є҆сѝ, ты̀ и҆ є҆диноро́дный

And as the Creed is being said,
the priest prays silently:

Prayer before the Kiss of Peace

O God and Master of all, make us, the unworthy, worthy of this holy hour in Thy
love for mankind, so that being cleansed from
every guile and every hypocrisy, we may be
united to one another by the bond of peace and
love, being established in the sanctification of
divine knowledge, through Thine only-begotten Son, our Lord and Saviour Jesus Christ,
with whom Thou art blessed, together with
Thine All-holy, good, and life-giving Spirit,
now and ever and unto ages of ages.

When the Creed is completed,
the deacon exclaims:

Let us stand well! In peace let us pray to the
Lord.

The priest says the exclamation:

For Thou art the God of peace, mercy, love,
compassion, and love for mankind, Thou and

тво́й сн҃ъ, и҆ дх҃ъ тво́й прест҃ы́й, ны́нѣ и҆ при́снѡ и҆ во вѣ́ки вѣкѡ́въ.

Ли́къ: А҆ми́нь.

Сщ҃е́нникъ: Ми́ръ всѣ́мъ.

Ли́къ: И҆ дꙋ́хови твоемꙋ̀.

Дїа́конъ: Возлю́бимъ дрꙋ́гъ дрꙋ́га лобза́нїемъ ст҃ы́мъ.

И҆ пою́тъ пѣ́вцы̀

ко́снѡ:

Возлюблю̀ тѧ̀, гдⷭ҇и, крѣ́посте моѧ̀, гдⷭ҇ь оу҆твержде́нїе, и҆ прибѣ́жище, и҆ и҆зба́витель мо́й.

И҆ цѣлꙋ́етъ сщ҃е́нникъ ст҃а̑ѧ пе́рвѣе верхꙋ̀ ст҃а́гѡ ді́скоса, та́же верхꙋ̀ ст҃а́гѡ поти́ра, и҆ кра́й ст҃ы́ѧ трапе́зы пре́дъ собо́ю. А҆́ще же бꙋ́дꙋтъ сщ҃е́нникѡвъ два̀, и҆лѝ мно́жае, то и҆ ѻ҆нѝ цѣлꙋ́ютъ ст҃а̑ѧ всѧ̑, и҆ дрꙋ́гъ дрꙋ́га, по ѡ҆бы́чаю. То́жде творѧ́тъ и҆ дїа́коны, стоѧ́ще на сѡлеѣ̀. По цѣлова́нїи же, возглаша́етъ дїа́конъ:

Главы̑ на́шѧ гдⷭ҇еви приклони́мъ.

Thine Only-begotten Son, and Thine All-holy Spirit, now and ever and unto the ages of ages.

SINGERS: Amen.

PRIEST: Peace be unto all.

SINGERS: And to thy spirit.

DEACON: Let us love one another with a holy kiss!

And the Singers chant slowly:

I will love Thee, O Lord, my strength; the Lord is my foundation, and my refuge and deliverer.

The priest kisses the gifts over the diskos and over the chalice, and the edge of the holy table before him. If there are two or more priests serving, they also kiss the gifts, and each other, according to the custom. The deacons do the same, standing on the solea. And after the giving of the kiss, the deacon says:

Let us bow our heads unto the Lord.

Ли́къ: Тебѣ̀, гд҃и.

Сщ҃е́нникъ, приклѡ́ньсѧ, мо́литсѧ та́йнѡ:

Е҆ди́ный гд҃и и҆ ми́лостивый бж҃е, приклонѧ́ющимъ своѧ̀ вы́ѧ пред̾ ст҃ы́мъ твои́мъ же́ртвенникомъ и҆ и҆щꙋ́щимъ ꙗ҆́же ѿ тебѐ дꙋхо́вныѧ да́ры, ниспослѝ бл҃года́ть твою̀ бл҃гꙋ́ю, и҆ бл҃гословѝ всѧ̀ ны̀ всѧ́кимъ бл҃гослове́нїемъ дꙋхо́вными и҆ неѿе́млемыми, и҆́же въ вы́шнихъ живы́й, и҆ на смире́нныѧ призира́й.

Возглаше́нїе:

Ꙗ҆́кѡ хва́льно и҆ покланѧ́емо и҆ препросла́влено е҆́сть пречестно́е и҆ великолѣ́пое и҆́мѧ твоѐ, ѻ҆ц҃а̀, и҆ сн҃а, и҆ ст҃а́гѡ дх҃а, ны́нѣ и҆ при́снѡ, и҆ во вѣ́ки вѣкѡ́въ.

Ли́къ: А҆ми́нь.

Нача́ло предложе́нїѧ ст҃а́гѡ и҆ требл҃же́ннагѡ і҆а́кѡва бра́та гд҃нѧ.

SINGERS: To Thee, O Lord.

The priest, bowing, says this prayer:

O only Lord and merciful God, send out Thy good grace upon those who bow their necks before Thy holy altar and who seek from Thee spiritual gifts, and bless us all with every spiritual blessing which cannot be taken away, Thou who dwellest on high and lookest down upon the humble.

Exclamation:

For praised and worshipped and glorified is Thine all-honorable and majestic holy Name: of the Father, and of the Son, and of the Holy Spirit, now and ever, and unto the ages of ages.

SINGERS: Amen.

The beginning of the Oblation of
the Holy and Thrice-blessed James
the Brother of the Lord

Дїа́конъ возглаша́етъ зрѧ́ще
къ ст҃ымъ две́ремъ:

Го́споди, бл҃гослови́.

И҆ вхо́дитъ во ст҃ый ѻ҆лта́рь.

Сщ҃е́нникъ глаго́летъ возгла́снѡ:

Гдⷭ҇ь да бл҃гослови́тъ и҆ ѡ҆ст҃и́тъ всѧ̀ ны̀ и҆
сослꙋ́житъ на́мъ и҆ досто́йны ны̀ сотвори́тъ
предстоѧ́нїѧ ст҃а́гѡ своегѡ̀ же́ртвенника и҆
прише́ствїѧ ст҃а́гѡ своегѡ̀ дх҃а, ны́нѣ и҆
при́снѡ и҆ во вѣ́ки вѣкѡ́въ.

Ли́къ, ко́снѡ:

А҆ми́нь.

Пѣвцє́мъ си́це пою́щымъ, сщ҃е́нникъ съ
сослꙋжа́щими покланѧ́етсѧ пред̾ ст҃о́ю
трапе́зою три́жды, гл҃юще въ себѣ̀:

Сла́ва въ вы́шнихъ бг҃ꙋ, и҆ на землѝ ми́ръ,
въ человѣ́цѣхъ бл҃говоле́нїе (г҃-жды).

Гдⷭ҇и, оу҆стнѣ̀ моѝ ѿве́рзеши, и҆ оу҆ста̀ моѧ̑
возвѣстѧ́тъ хвалꙋ̀ твою̀ (г҃-жды).

Да и҆спо́лнѧтсѧ оу҆ста̀ моѧ̑ хвале́нїѧ твоегѡ̀

The deacon exclaims, looking toward
the holy doors:

Lord, bless.

And he enters the sanctuary.

The priest says aloud:

May the Lord bless and sanctify all of us, and
may He minister with us and make us worthy
of standing before His holy altar, and of the
coming of his Holy Spirit, now and ever and
unto the ages of ages.

The singers chant slowly:

Amen.

While the singers chant this, the priest,
with the concelebrants, bows before the
holy table, saying this within himself:

Glory to God in the highest, and on earth
peace, good will among men (thrice).
O Lord, Thou shalt open my lips and my
mouth shall declare Thy praise (thrice).
Let my mouth be filled with Thy praise, O

гд҃и, ꙗ҆́кѡ да воспою̀ сла́вꙋ твою̀, ве́сь де́нь
великолѣ́пїе твоѐ (г҃-жды).

И҆ присовокꙋпля́етъ:

Ѻ҆ц҃а̀, и҆ сн҃а, и҆ ста́гѡ дх҃а, ны́нѣ и҆ при́снѡ,
и҆ во вѣ́ки вѣкѡ́въ, а҆ми́нь.

И҆ поклони́вшесѧ ма́лѡ на ѻ҆́бѣ страны̀
сто́й трапе́зы, пое́тъ вкꙋ́пѣ
съ сослꙋжа́щими:

Возвели́чите гд҃а со мно́ю, и҆ вознесе́мъ
и҆́мѧ є҆гѡ̀ вкꙋ́пѣ.

Ли́къ же ѿвѣща́етъ:

Дх҃ъ ст҃ы́й на́йдетъ на тѧ̀, и҆ си́ла
вы́шнѧгѡ ѡ҆сѣни́тъ тѧ̀.

Сослꙋжа́щїи и҆лѝ є҆ди́нъ дїа́конъ:

Помѧнѝ и҆ на́съ, влады́ко.

И҆ сщ҃е́нникъ гл҃етъ:

Да помѧне́тъ ва́съ гд҃ь во цр҃твїи небе́снѣмъ
всегда̀, ны́нѣ и҆ при́снѡ и҆ во вѣ́ки
вѣкѡ́въ.

Lord, that I may sing unto Thy glory and all day unto Thy majesty (thrice).

And then he adds:
Of the Father, and of the Son, and of the Holy Spirit, now and ever and unto the ages of ages. Amen.

And, making small bows to both sides of the holy table, he sings together with the concelebrating priests:
O magnify the Lord with me, and let us exalt His Name together.

And the singers respond:
The Holy Spirit shall come upon thee and the power of the Most High shall overshadow thee.

The concelebrants or the deacon alone:
Remember us also, master.

And the priest says:
May the Lord remember you in the heavenly Kingdom, always, now and ever and unto the ages of ages.

Дїа́конъ гл҃етъ а҆ми́нь, и҆сходитъ и҆зъ
ст҃а́гѡ Ѻ҆лтарѧ̀ и҆ гл҃етъ собо́рнꙋю е҆кте́нїю,
ста́въ на ѻ҆бы́чнѣмъ мѣ́стѣ. Глаго́лемымъ
дїа́конствамъ си́мъ, глаго́летъ сщ҃е́нникъ
моли́твы та́йнѡ, ли́стъ 96.

Ми́ромъ гдⷭ҇ꙋ помо́лимсѧ.

Ли́къ: Гдⷭ҇и поми́лꙋй.

Спасѝ, поми́лꙋй, оу҆ще́дри, оу҆слы́ши,
застꙋпѝ и҆ сохранѝ на́съ бж҃е, тво́ею
бл҃года́тїю.

Ли́къ: Гдⷭ҇и поми́лꙋй.

Ѡ҆ свы́шнемъ ми́рѣ и҆ бж҃їи чл҃вѣколю́бїи,
ѡ҆ е҆диномы́слїи и҆ сп҃се́нїи дꙋ́шъ на́шихъ,
гдⷭ҇ꙋ помо́лимсѧ.

Ли́къ: Гдⷭ҇и поми́лꙋй.

Ѡ҆ ми́рѣ всегѡ̀ мі́ра, и҆ ѡ҆ соедине́нїи
ст҃ы́хъ бж҃їихъ правосла́вныхъ цр҃кве́й, гдⷭ҇ꙋ
помо́лимсѧ.

Ли́къ: Гдⷭ҇и поми́лꙋй.

Ѡ҆ е҆ди́нѣй ст҃ѣ́й собо́рнѣй и҆ а҆пⷧльстѣ́й
цр҃кви, ꙗ҆́же ѿ конє́цъ землѝ да́же до
конє́цъ ꙗ҆̀, гдⷭ҇ꙋ помо́лимсѧ.

The deacon says Amen, exits the sanctuary, and says the catholic litany, standing at the usual place. While this litany is being said, the priest says silently the prayers on p. 97.

In peace let us pray to the Lord.

SINGERS: Lord have mercy.

Save us, have mercy on us, be compassionate to us, hear us, help us, and keep us, O God, by Thy grace.

SINGERS: Lord have mercy.

For the peace from above and the love of God for mankind, for oneness of mind and the salvation of our souls, let us pray to the Lord.

SINGERS: Lord have mercy.

For the peace of the whole world and for the union of all the holy Orthodox churches of God, let us pray to the Lord.

SINGERS: Lord have mercy.

For the one holy, catholic and apostolic Church which abideth from one end of the earth to the other end, let us pray to the Lord.

Ли́къ: Гдⷭ҇и поми́лꙋй.

Ѡ҆ спⷭ҇е́нїи и҆ застꙋпле́нїи ст҃а́гѡ ѻ҆тца̀ на́шегѡ, а҆рхїепⷭ҇копа (и҆лѝ митрополі́та) и҆́мⷬ҇къ, ѡ҆ все́мъ при́чтѣ и҆ хрⷭ҇толюби́выхъ лю́дехъ, гдⷭ҇ꙋ помо́лимсѧ.

Ли́къ: Гдⷭ҇и, поми́лꙋй.

Ѡ҆ бг҃охрани́мѣй странѣ̀ се́й, власте́хъ и҆ во́инствѣ є҆ѧ̀, гдⷭ҇ꙋ помо́лимсѧ.

Ли́къ: Гдⷭ҇и, поми́лꙋй.

Ѡ҆ ст҃ѣ́мъ гра́дѣ бг҃а на́шегѡ, ѡ҆ ца́рствꙋющемъ гра́дѣ, ѡ҆ гра́дѣ се́мъ (и҆лѝ ѡ҆ ве́си се́й, и҆лѝ ѡ҆ ст҃е́й ѻ҆би́тели се́й) и҆ ѡ҆ всѧ́комъ гра́дѣ и҆ странѣ̀, и҆ ѡ҆ и҆́хже правосла́вною вѣ́рою и҆ блг҃оче́стїемъ живꙋ́щихъ въ ни́хъ, ѡ҆ ми́рѣ и҆ сохране́нїи и҆́хъ, гдⷭ҇ꙋ помо́лимсѧ.

Ли́къ: Гдⷭ҇и, поми́лꙋй.

Ѡ҆ плодоносѧ́щихъ и҆ добродѣ́ющихъ во ст҃ы́хъ бж҃їихъ це́рквахъ, и҆ ѡ҆ помина́ющихъ ѹ҆бѡ́гїѧ, вдови́цы и҆ си́рыѧ, стра́нныѧ и҆ въ нꙋ́ждѣ сꙋ́щыѧ, и҆ ѡ҆ заповѣ́давшихъ

SINGERS: Lord have mercy.

For the salvation and protection of our holy father, Archbishop [or Metropolitan] N., for all the clergy and the Christ-loving people, let us pray to the Lord.

SINGERS: Lord have mercy.

For this God-preserved land, its authorities and armed forces, let us pray to the Lord.

SINGERS: Lord have mercy.

For the holy city of Christ our God, and the royal city, this city [or: village, or: holy monastery] and every city and countryside, and for those who in Orthodox faith and piety dwell therein, and for their peace and safety, let us pray to the Lord.

SINGERS: Lord have mercy.

For those who bring offerings and do good works in the holy churches of God and for those who remember the poor, the widows and the orphans, the strangers and the needy, and for those who have commanded

на́мъ ꙗ́кш да помина́ти и҆́хъ въ мл҃твахъ,
гдУ помо́лимсѧ.

Ли́къ: Гд҃и, поми́лУй.

Ѽ хрⷭ҇тїа́нѣхъ, приходѧ́щихъ и҆ гра-
дУ́щихъ поклони́тисѧ во ст҃ы́хъ хрⷭ҇та̀ бг҃а
на́шегш мѣ́стѣхъ си́хъ, ѡ пла́вающихъ,
пУтеше́ствУющихъ, стра́нствУющихъ, и҆ въ
плѣне́нїи сУ́щихъ бра́тїахъ на́шихъ, ѡ ми́рномъ
возвраще́нїи коегш́ждо и҆́хъ съ ра́достїю
вско́рѣ во своѧ̀ сн҃, гдУ помо́лимсѧ.

Ли́къ: Гд҃и, поми́лУй.

Ѽ въ ста́рости и҆ въ не́мощи сУ́щихъ,
болѧ́щихъ, трУжда́ющихсѧ, и҆ ѡ дУ́хшвъ
нечи́стыхъ стУжа́емыхъ, и҆ ѡ и҆́же ѡ бг҃а
ско́ромъ и҆сцѣле́нїи и҆ спасе́нїи и҆́хъ, гдУ
помо́лимсѧ.

Ли́къ: Гд҃и, поми́лУй.

И҆ ѡ всѧ́кой дУшѝ хрⷭ҇тїа́нстѣй, скор-
бѧ́щей же и҆ ѡзло́бленнѣй, ми́лости бж҃їей
и҆ по́мощи требУ́ющей, и҆ ѡ ѡбраще́нїи забл У́-
дшихъ, и҆сцѣле́нїи болѧ́щихъ, свобожде́нїи
плѣне́нныхъ, оу҆поко́енїи преждепочи́вшихъ
Ѻ҆те́цъ и҆ бра́тїй на́шихъ, гдУ помо́лимсѧ.

us to remember them in our prayer, let us pray to the Lord.

SINGERS: Lord have mercy.

For the Christians who have come and those who draw near to worship in these holy places of Christ our God, for those who sail, for those who travel and dwell abroad, and our brothers in captivity, for the peaceful and speedy return of each one of them to their homes with joy, let us pray to the Lord.

SINGERS: Lord have mercy.

For the aged and the infirm, the sick, the weary, and for those who are vexed by unclean spirits, and for their speedy healing from God and their salvation, let us pray to the Lord.

SINGERS: Lord have mercy.

And for every Christian soul that is afflicted and tormented, in need of mercy and help from God; and for the conversion of the deceived, the healing of the sick, the liberation of captives, and for the repose of our fathers and brethren gone to rest before us, let us pray to the Lord.

Ли́къ: Гдⷭ҇и, поми́лꙋй.

Ѡ҆ и҆̀же въ дѣ́вствѣ и҆ чистотѣ́ и҆ по́стничествѣ и҆ въ сщⷭ҇е́ннѣмъ бра́цѣ пребыва́ющихъ, и҆ ѡ҆ и҆̀хже въ гора́хъ, верте́пахъ и҆ про́пастѣхъ земны́хъ подвиза́ющихсѧ преподо́бныхъ Ѻ҆тцѣ́хъ и҆ бра́тїахъ на́шихъ, гдⷭ҇ꙋ помо́лимсѧ.

Ли́къ: Гдⷭ҇и, поми́лꙋй.

Ѡ҆ предстоѧ́щихъ и҆ молѧ́щихсѧ съ на́ми въ ст҃ы́й се́й ча́съ и҆ на всѧ́кое вре́мѧ Ѻ҆тцѣ́хъ же и҆ бра́тїахъ, ѡ҆ тща́нїи, трꙋдѣ́ и҆ ѹ҆се́рдїи и҆̀хъ, гдⷭ҇ꙋ помо́лимсѧ.

Ли́къ: Гдⷭ҇и, поми́лꙋй.

Ѡ҆ ѡ҆ставле́нїи грѣхѡ́въ и҆ проще́нїи прегрѣше́нїй на́шихъ, и҆ ѡ҆ и҆зба́витисѧ и҆ спⷭ҇ти́сѧ на́мъ ѿ всѧ́кїѧ ско́рби, гнѣ́ва и҆ нꙋ́жды и҆ воста́нїѧ ꙗ҆зы́кѡвъ, гдⷭ҇ꙋ помо́лимсѧ.

Ли́къ: Гдⷭ҇и, поми́лꙋй.

Ѡ҆ бл҃горастворе́нїи воздꙋ́хѡвъ, дожде́хъ ми́рныхъ, ро́сахъ бл҃ги́хъ и҆ бл҃гослове́нныхъ, плодѡ́въ и҆зоби́лїи, соверше́нномъ плодоро́дїи и҆ ѡ҆ вѣнцѣ́ лѣ́та, гдⷭ҇ꙋ помо́лимсѧ.

SINGERS: Lord have mercy.

For those who lead their lives in virginity, purity, asceticism, and in holy matrimony; and for our venerable fathers and brethren who struggle in mountains, caverns, and pits of the earth, let us pray to the Lord.

SINGERS: Lord have mercy.

For our fathers and brethren who are present and who pray with us at this holy hour and at all times, for their diligence, labor, and zeal, let us pray to the Lord.

SINGERS: Lord have mercy.

For the remission of our sins and forgiveness of our offenses, and for our deliverance and salvation from all tribulation, wrath, and necessity, and from uprisings of the nations, let us pray to the Lord.

SINGERS: Lord have mercy.

For seasonable weather, peaceful rains, good and blessed dews, abundance of fruits, a full harvest, and the crown of the year, let us pray to the Lord.

Ли́къ: Гд҃и, поми́лꙋй.

Ѡ҆ є҆́же ѹ҆слы́шатисѧ и҆ бл҃гопрїѧ́тнꙋ бы́ти моле́нїю на́шемꙋ пре́дъ бг҃омъ, и҆ низпосла́тисѧ бога́тымъ ми́лостемъ и҆ ще́дротамъ є҆гѡ̀ на всѧ̀ ны̀ и҆ ѡ҆ сподо́битисѧ на́мъ црⷭ҇твїа нбⷭ҇нагѡ, приле́жнѡ помо́лимсѧ.

Ли́къ: Гд҃и, поми́лꙋй.

Прест҃ꙋ́ю и҆ пребл҃гослове́ннꙋю, пречⷭ҇тꙋ́ю влⷣчцꙋ на́шꙋ бцⷣꙋ и҆ приснодв҃ꙋ мр҃і́ю, честны́ѧ безпло́тныѧ а҆рха́ггелы, ст҃а́го і҆ѡа́нна, сла́внаго пррⷪ҇ка, пртⷱ҇чꙋ и҆ крⷭ҇ти́телѧ, бж҃е́ственныѧ, сщ҃е́нныѧ а҆п҃лы, прⷪ҇ро́ки и҆ страстоте́рпцы мч҃ники, и҆ ст҃а́го и҆ бл҃же́ннаго ѻ҆тца̀ на́шего і҆а́кѡва а҆п҃ла и҆ бра́та бж҃їѧ, стефа́на протодїа́кона и҆ первомч҃ника, и҆ всѧ̀ ст҃ы́ѧ и҆ пра́ведныѧ помѧне́мъ, ꙗ҆́кѡ да мл҃твами и҆ предста́тельствы и҆́хъ всѝ поми́лованы бꙋ́демъ.

Ли́къ: Гд҃и, поми́лꙋй.

И҆ ѡ҆ предложе́нныхъ ст҃ы́хъ, сла́вныхъ, небе́сныхъ, та́йныхъ, стра́шныхъ, чтⷭ҇ны́хъ,

SINGERS: Lord have mercy.

That our prayer may be heard and become acceptable before God, and that His abundant mercies and compassion may be sent down upon us all, and that we may be vouchsafed the heavenly kingdom, let us fervently pray.

SINGERS: Lord have mercy.

Let us call to remembrance our most holy, most blessed, and most pure Lady Theotokos and Ever-Virgin Mary, the honorable bodiless archangels, the holy glorious Prophet, Forerunner, and Baptist John, the divine and sacred apostles, prophets, and passion-bearing martyrs, and our holy and blessed father James the Apostle and the Brother of the Lord, the Protodeacon and First Martyr Stephen, and all the saints and righteous ones, so that by their intercessions and protection we all may receive mercy.

SINGERS: Lord have mercy.

And for the holy, glorious, heavenly, mystical, dreadful, precious, divine gifts that are

бж҃е́ственныхъ дарѣ́хъ, и҆ ѡ҆ спасе́ніи предстоѧ́щагѡ и҆ приносѧ́щагѡ а҃ ст҃а́гѡ ѻ҆тца̀ на́шегѡ и҆ а҆рхїере́а (и҆лѝ а҆рхїмандрі́та и҆лѝ і҆ере́а) и҆́мк҃ъ, гд҃а бг҃а на́шегѡ мо́лимъ.

Ли́къ: Гд҃и, поми́лꙋй (г҃_жды).

Глаго́лемымъ же дїа́конствамъ си̑мъ, мо́литсѧ сщ҃е́нникъ пред̾ ст҃о́ю трапе́зою, преклони́въ главꙋ̀ та́йнѡ си́це:

По҆сѣти́вый на́съ ми́лостїю и҆ щедро́тами, вл҃ко гд҃и, и҆ дарова́вый дерзнове́нїе на́мъ, смире́ннымъ и҆ грѣ́шнымъ и҆ недосто́йнымъ рабѡ́мъ твои́мъ предстоѧ́ти ст҃о́мꙋ твоемꙋ̀ же́ртвенникꙋ и҆ приноси́ти тебѣ̀ стра́шнꙋю сїю̀ и҆ безкро́внꙋю же́ртвꙋ ѡ҆ на́шихъ грѣсѣ́хъ и҆ ѡ҆ людски́хъ невѣ́дѣнїихъ, при́зри на мѧ̀, непотре́бнагѡ раба̀ твоегѡ̀, и҆ простѝ моѧ̑ согрѣше́нїѧ твои́мъ бл҃гоꙋтро́бїемъ, и҆ ѡ҆чи́сти мѝ ꙋ҆стнѣ̀ и҆ се́рдце ѿ всѧ́кїѧ скве́рны пло́ти и҆ дх҃а, и҆ ѿста́ви ѿ менѐ всѧ́кїй по́мыслъ сра́мный же и҆ неразꙋ́мный, и҆ ꙋ҆дово́ли мѧ̀, си́лою всест҃а́гѡ твоегѡ̀ дх҃а въ слꙋ́жбꙋ сїю̀, и҆ прїими́ мѧ ра́ди

offered, and for the salvation of our holy father and hierarch [or: archimandrite or: priest] N. who presides and offers them, let us entreat the Lord our God.

SINGERS: Lord have mercy (thrice).

While this litany is said, the priest stands before the holy altar and bowing his head, says these prayers within himself:

O Master Lord who hast visited us with mercy and compassion, and hast granted to us, thy humble, sinful, and unworthy servants, boldness to stand before Thy holy altar and to offer Thee this dread and bloodless sacrifice for our sins and for the sins of the ignorance of the people: look down upon me, Thine unprofitable servant, and blot out my transgressions on account of Thy tender mercy, and cleanse my lips and heart from every defilement of flesh and spirit, and remove from me every shameful and irrational thought, and by the power of Thine All-holy Spirit make me sufficient for this liturgy, and accept me for the

твоеѧ̀ бл҃гости, приближа́ющагосѧ ст҃о́мꙋ
твоемꙋ̀ же́ртвенникꙋ, и҆ бл҃говоли̂, гдⷭ҇и,
прїѧ́тнымъ бы́ти приноси́мымъ тебѣ̀
дарѡ́мъ си̂мъ рꙋка́ми на́шими, снисходѧ́ще
мои̂мъ не́мощемъ, и҆ не ѿве́ржи менѐ ѿ
лица̀ твоегѡ̀, нижѐ возгнꙋша́йсѧ моегѡ̀
недосто́инства, но помилꙋ́й мѧ̀ бж҃е, по
вели́цѣй ми́лости твое́й, и҆ по мно́жествꙋ
щедро́тъ твои́хъ пре́зри беззакѡ́нїѧ моѧ̑,
ꙗ҆́кѡ да неѡсꙋжде́ннѡ прише́дъ пре́дъ
ст҃о́ю сла́вою твое́ю, сподо́блюсѧ покро́ва
є҆диноро́днагѡ твоегѡ̀ сн҃а и҆ ѡ҆сїѧ́нїѧ
прест҃а́гѡ твоегѡ̀ дх҃а, и҆ не ꙗ҆́кѡ ра́бъ
грѣха̀ ѿве́рженъ бꙋ́дꙋ, но ꙗ҆́кѡ ра́бъ тво́й
ѡ҆брѣтꙋ̀ бл҃года́ть и҆ ми́лость и҆ ѡ҆ставле́нїе
грѣхѡ́въ, въ се́мъ и҆ бꙋ́дꙋщемъ вѣ́цѣ. є҆́й,
влⷣко вседержи́телю, всеси́льне гдⷭ҇и, оу҆слы́ши
моле́нїе моѐ: ты̀ бо є҆сѝ всѧ̀ дѣ́йствꙋѧй во
всѣ́хъ, и҆ ѿ тебѐ всѝ ча́емъ во всѣ́хъ по́мощи
же и҆ застꙋпле́нїѧ, и҆ ѿ є҆диноро́днагѡ
твоегѡ̀ сн҃а и҆ животворѧ́щагѡ дх҃а, ны́нѣ
и҆ при́снѡ, и҆ во вѣ́ки вѣкѡ́въ, а҆ми́нь.

sake of Thy goodness as I approach Thy holy al-tar, and be well-pleased, O Lord, condescend-ing to my weakness, that these gifts which are brought forth by our hands may be acceptable, and cast me not away from thy face, neither abhor mine unworthiness, but have mercy on me, O God, according to Thy great mercy, and according to the multitude of Thy compassion pass over my transgressions, that having en-tered without condemnation before Thy holy glory, I may be made worthy of the protection of Thine only-begotten Son and the illumina-tion of Thine All-holy Spirit; and may I not be cast out as a slave of sin, but as Thy servant may I find grace and mercy and remission of the sins in this age and in the age to come. Yea, almighty Master, all-powerful Lord, hearken to my prayer, for Thou art He that works all things in all, and we seek assistance and help in all things from Thee, and from Thine only-be-gotten Son and thy life-giving Spirit, now and ever and unto the ages of ages. Amen.

И҆ мл҃твꙋ сїю̀:

Б҃же и҆́же мно́гагѡ ра́ди и҆ неи҆зрече́ннагѡ чл҃вѣколю́бїа посла́вый є҆диноро́днаго твоего̀ сн҃а въ мі́ръ, да заблꙋ́ждшее возврати́тъ ѻ҆вча̀, не ѿврати́сѧ на́съ грѣ́шныхъ дерза́ющихъ приноси́ти тебѣ̀ сїю̀ стра́шнꙋю и҆ безкро́внꙋю же́ртвꙋ: не бо на пра́вды на́ша ᲂу҆пова́емъ, но на ми́лость твою̀ бл҃гꙋ́ю, є҆́юже ро́дъ на́шъ соблюда́еши. и҆ ны́нѣ мо́лимъ и҆ про́симъ твою̀ бл҃гостꙋ́ню: да не бꙋ́детъ во ѡ҆сꙋжде́нїе лю́демъ твои҆́мъ ᲂу҆гото́ванное на́мъ сїѐ ко спасе́нїю та́инство, но во ѡ҆ставле́нїе грѣхѡ́въ, во ѡ҆бновле́нїе дꙋ́шъ и҆ тѣле́съ, во бл҃гоᲂу҆гожде́нїе тебѣ̀, бг҃ꙋ и҆ ѻ҆ц҃ꙋ.

И҆ мл҃твꙋ сїю̀,
ст҃а́гѡ васі́лїа:

Г҃ди бж҃е на́шъ, созда́вый на́съ, и҆ введы́й въ жи́знь сїю̀, показа́вый на́мъ пꙋти̑ во спасе́нїе, дарова́вый на́мъ небе́ныхъ та́ннъ ѿкрове́нїе: ты̀ бо є҆сѝ положи́вый

And this prayer:

O God who through Thy great and ineffable love for mankind didst send Thine Only-begotten Son into the world, that He might turn back the sheep that had gone astray, turn not away from us sinners who dare to offer Thee this fearsome and bloodless sacrifice. For we trust not in our own righteousness, but in Thy good mercy, by which Thou dost preserve our race. And now we supplicate and beseech Thy goodness that this mystery prepared for our salvation may not be unto condemnation for Thy people, but for the removal of sins, for the renewal of souls and bodies, for the good pleasure of Thee, God and Father.

And this Prayer of St Basil the Great:

O Lord our God, who hast created us and brought us into this life; who hast shown us the ways to salvation, and bestowed on us the revelation of heavenly mysteries: it

на́съ въ слꙋ́жбꙋ сїю̀, си́лою дх҃а твоегѡ̀
ст҃а́гѡ. бл҃говолѝ ᲂу҆́бѡ гдⷭ҇и, бы́ти на́мъ
слꙋжи́телемъ но́вагѡ твоегѡ̀ завѣ́та,
слꙋга́мъ ст҃ы́хъ твои́хъ та́инствъ, прїимѝ
на́съ приближа́ющихсѧ ст҃о́мꙋ твоемꙋ̀
же́ртвенникꙋ, по мно́жествꙋ ми́лости
твоеѧ̀, да бꙋ́демъ досто́йни приноси́ти
тебѣ̀ слове́снꙋю сїю̀ и҆ безкро́внꙋю же́ртвꙋ
ѡ҆ на́шихъ согрѣше́нїихъ и҆ ѡ҆ людски́хъ
невѣ́жествіихъ: ю҆́же прїе́мъ во ст҃ый и҆
пренебе́сный, и҆ мы́сленный тво́й же́ртвенникъ,
въ воню̀ бл҃гоꙋха́нїѧ, возниспослѝ на́мъ
бл҃года́ть ст҃а́гѡ твоегѡ̀ дх҃а. при́зри на ны̀
бж҃е, и҆ ви́ждь на слꙋ́жбꙋ сїю̀ на́шꙋ, и҆ прїимѝ
ю҆̀, ꙗ҆́коже прїѧ́лъ є҆сѝ а҆́велевы да́ры, нѡ́евы
же́ртвы, а҆враа́мова всепло́дїѧ, мѡѷсе́ова
и҆ а҆арѡ́нова сщ҃е́нства, самꙋ́илова ми́рнаѧ.
ꙗ҆́коже прїѧ́лъ є҆сѝ ѿ ст҃ы́хъ твои́хъ а҆пⷭ҇лъ
и҆́стиннꙋю сїю̀ слꙋ́жбꙋ, си́це и҆ ѿ рꙋ́къ на́съ
грѣ́шныхъ прїимѝ да́ры сїѧ̀ въ бл҃гости
твое́й гдⷭ҇и: ꙗ҆́кѡ да сподо́бльшесѧ слꙋжи́ти
без̾ поро́ка ст҃о́мꙋ твоемꙋ̀ же́ртвенникꙋ,

is Thou who hast appointed us to this service by the power of Thy Holy Spirit. Therefore, O Lord, enable us to be ministers of Thy New Covenant and servants of Thy Holy Mysteries. Through the greatness of Thy mercy, accept us as we draw near to Thy holy altar, so that we may be worthy to offer to Thee this rational and bloodless sacrifice for our sins and for the errors of Thy people. Having received it upon Thy holy and noetic altar above the heavens as an odor of good fragrance, do Thou send down upon us the grace of Thy Holy Spirit. Look down on us, O God, and behold this our service. Receive it as Thou didst receive the gifts of Abel, the sacrifices of Noah, the whole-burnt offerings of Abraham, the priestly offices of Moses and Aaron, and the peace-offerings of Samuel. Even as Thou didst receive from Thy holy apostles this true worship, so now, in Thy goodness, accept these gifts from the hands of us sinners, O Lord; that having been accounted

ѡ҆бра́щемъ мздꙋ̀ вѣ́рныхъ и҆ мꙋ́дрыхъ
строи́телей въ де́нь стра́шный воздаѧ́нїѧ
твоегѡ̀ пра́веднагѡ и҆ бл҃га́гѡ.

Та́же гл҃етъ сщ҃е́нникъ
мл҃твꙋ завѣ́сы:

Бл҃годари́мъ тѧ̀ гд҃и бж҃е на́шъ, ꙗ҆́кѡ да́лъ
є҆сѝ на́мъ дерзнове́нїе входи́ти во ст҃а̑ѧ
кро́вїю і҆и҃совою, є҆́же ѡ҆бнови́лъ є҆сѝ на́мъ
пꙋ́ть но́вый и҆ живы́й завѣ́сою пло́ти є҆гѡ̀:
сподо́бльшесѧ же вни́ти въ мѣ́сто селе́нїѧ
сла́вы твоеѧ̀, внꙋ́трь же бы́ти завѣ́сы, и҆
ст҃а̑ѧ ст҃ы́хъ зрѣ́ти, припа́даемъ бл҃гостꙑ́ни
твое́й, влⷣко, поми́лꙋй на́съ, поне́же
пристра́шни є҆смы̀ и҆ притре́петны, хотѧ́ще
предстоѧ́ти ст҃о́мꙋ твоемꙋ̀ же́ртвенникꙋ: и҆
ѡ҆блека́ющїѧ сщ҃еннодѣ́йствїе сїѐ ѡ҆бра́знѡ
покро́вы гада́нїй ѿкры́въ, свѣ́тлѡ на́мъ
покажѝ и҆ ᲂу҆́мнаѧ на́ша о҆́чи неѡб̾ꙗ́тнагѡ
твоегѡ̀ свѣ́та и҆спо́лни и҆ ѡ҆чи́стивъ
нищетꙋ̀ на́шꙋ ѿ всѧ́кїѧ скве́рны пло́ти
и҆ дꙋ́ха, досто́йнꙋ ю҆̀ содѣ́лай стра́шнагѡ
сегѡ̀ и҆ ᲂу҆жа́снагѡ предстоѧ́нїѧ, ꙗ҆́кѡ

worthy to serve without offence at Thy holy altar, we may receive the reward of wise and faithful stewards on the dread day of Thy just and good retribution.

Then the priest says the Prayer of the Veil:

We give thanks unto Thee, O Lord our God, that Thou hast given us boldness to enter into the holy place by the blood of Jesus, which Thou hast renewed unto us as a new and living way through the veil of His flesh. Having thus been made worthy to enter into the dwelling-place of Thy glory and to come inside the veil and to behold the holy of holies, we fall down before Thy goodness, Master: have mercy on us! For we are fearful and trembling as we are about to stand before Thy holy altar. And, having uncovered the veils of figures which symbolically envelop this sacred mystery, do Thou show it clearly unto us, and fill the eyes of our mind with Thy boundless light; and having cleansed our lowliness from every defilement of flesh

преблгоꙋтро́бенъ и҆ ми́лостивъ бг҃ъ є҆сѝ, и҆
тебѣ̀ сла́вꙋ и҆ бл҃годаре́нїе возсыла́емъ, и҆
є҆диноро́дномꙋ твоемꙋ̀ сн҃ꙋ, и҆ прест҃о́мꙋ и҆
бл҃го́мꙋ и҆ животворѧ́щемꙋ твоемꙋ̀ дх҃ꙋ,
нн҃ѣ и҆ при́снѡ и҆ во вѣ́ки вѣкѡ́въ,
а҆ми́нь.

И҆ па́ки мо́литсѧ сщ҃е́нникъ
ѡ҆ себѣ̀, гл҃ѧ:

Бл҃гі́й и҆ чл҃вѣколю́бче гдⷭ҇и, и҆́же
при́ше́ствїемъ є҆диноро́днагѡ твоегѡ̀
сн҃а и҆ возсїѧ́нїемъ ст҃а́гѡ твоегѡ̀ дх҃а,
сподо́билъ мѧ̀ є҆сѝ грѣ́шнаго и҆ недосто́йнаго
раба̀ твоего̀ предстоѧ́ти ст҃о́мꙋ твоемꙋ̀
же́ртвенникꙋ и҆ приноси́ти и҆ слꙋжи́ти
пречи́стымъ но́вагѡ завѣ́та твоегѡ̀
та́йнамъ, сподо́би мѧ̀ чи́стою со́вѣстїю
слꙋжи́ти тебѣ̀ всѧ̑ дни̑ живота̀ моегѡ̀.

Сконча́вшимсѧ же дїа́конствамъ си̑мъ,
сщ҃е́нникъ гл҃етъ возглаше́нїе сїѐ:

Ми́лостїю и҆ щедро́тами и҆ чл҃вѣколю́бїемъ
є҆диноро́днагѡ сн҃а твоегѡ̀, съ ни́мже

and spirit, make us worthy of this fearful and dread ministry, for Thou art a most compassionate and merciful God and unto Thee do we send up glory and thanksgiving, to Thine only-begotten Son and to Thine All-holy, good, and life-giving Spirit, now and ever and unto ages of ages.

And he further prays for himself, saying:

O good Lord who lovest mankind, who by the coming of Thine only-begotten Son and the enlightenment of Thy Holy Spirit hast vouchsafed me, Thy sinful and unworthy servant, to stand before Thy holy altar and to offer and to celebrate the immaculate mysteries of Thy New Covenant, make me worthy to worship Thee with a pure conscience all the days of my life.

When the deacon has finished these petitions, the priest says this exclamation:

Through the mercies and compassions and love for mankind of Thine only-begotten Son,

бл҃гословéнъ є҆сѝ, и҆ со прест҃ы́мъ и҆ бл҃гимъ и҆ живоворѧ́щимъ твои́мъ дх҃омъ, ны́нѣ и҆ при́снѡ и҆ во вѣ́ки вѣкѡ́въ.

Ли́къ: А҆ми́нь.

Сщ҃éнникъ: Ми́ръ всѣ́мъ.

Ли́къ: И҆ ду́хови твоему̀.

Діа́конъ:

С
та́немъ добрѣ̀: ста́немъ бл҃гочéстнѣ. Ста́немъ со стра́хомъ бж҃íимъ и҆ сокру́шéнїемъ. во́нмемъ ст҃о́му возношéнїю въ мíрѣ бг҃у приноси́ти.

Ли́къ: Ми́лость, ми́ръ, жéртву хвалéнїѧ.

Сщ҃éнникъ бл҃гословлѧ́етъ, возглаша́ѧ:

Л
юбы̀ бг҃а и҆ ѻ҆ц҃à, и҆ бл҃года́ть гд҃а и҆ бг҃а и҆ спа́са на́шегѡ і҆и҃са хрⷭ҇та̀ и҆ причáстїе и҆ да́ръ прест҃а́гѡ дх҃а бу́ди со всѣ́ми ва́ми.

Ли́къ: И҆ со ду́хомъ твои́мъ.

Сщ҃éнникъ: Горѣ̀ и҆мѣ́имъ о҆у҆́мъ и҆ сердца̀.

Ли́къ: И҆́мамы ко гд҃у.

Сщ҃éнникъ: Бл҃годари́мъ гд҃а.

with whom Thou art blessed, together with
Thine All-holy, good, and life-giving Spirit,
now and ever and unto the ages of ages.

SINGERS: Amen.

PRIEST: Peace be unto all.

SINGERS: And to thy spirit.

Deacon:

Let us stand well, let us stand piously, let us
stand with the fear of God and compunc-
tion. Let us attend to the holy oblation, to offer it to God in peace.

SINGERS: Mercy, peace, a sacrifice of praise.

The priest blesses, exclaiming:

The love of God and Father, and the grace
of our Lord, God, and Saviour Jesus
Christ, and the communion and gift of the
Most-holy Spirit, be with you all.

SINGERS: And with thy spirit.

PRIEST: Let us lift up our mind and hearts.

SINGERS: We lift them up unto the Lord.

PRIEST: Let us give thanks unto the Lord.

Ли́къ: досто́йнѡ и҆ пра́веднѡ.

Сщ҃е́нникъ приклони́въ главꙋ̀, начина́етъ
гл҃а́ти мл҃твꙋ ст҃а́гѡ возноше́нїѧ:

Ꙗ҆́кѡ вои́стинꙋ досто́йнѡ є҆́сть и҆
пра́веднѡ, подо́бно же и҆ до́лжно, тебѣ̀
хвали́ти, тебѣ̀ пѣ́ти, тебѣ̀ бл҃гослови́ти,
тебѣ̀ славосло́вити, тебѣ̀ бл҃годари́ти,
всеѧ̀ тва́ри, ви́димыѧ же и҆ неви́димыѧ
содѣ́тела, сокро́вище вѣ́чныхъ бл҃гъ,
и҆сто́чника жи́зни и҆ безсме́ртїѧ, всѣ́хъ бг҃а
и҆ влⷣкꙋ, є҆го́же пою́тъ небеса̀ и҆ небеса̀ небе́съ,
и҆ всѧ̑ си́лы и҆́хъ, со́лнце же и҆ лꙋна̀ и҆ ве́сь
ѕвѣ́здный ли́къ, землѧ̀, мо́ре, и҆ всѧ̑ ꙗ҆̀же
въ ни́хъ, і҆ерⷭли́мъ пренебе́сный, торжество̀
и҆збра́нныхъ, цр҃ковь перворо́дныхъ, напи̑-
санныхъ на небесѣ́хъ, дꙋ́си пра́ведныхъ и҆
прⷪро́къ, дꙋ́ши мч҃еникъ и҆ а҆п҃лъ, а҆́гг҃ели,
а҆рха́гг҃ели, престо́ли, гдⷭтвїѧ, нача́ла же и҆
вла́сти, си́лы стра́шныѧ, херꙋві́ми мно́го-
очи́тїи, и҆ шестокрыла́ти серафі́ми, ꙗ҆̀же
ᲂу҆́бѡ двѣма̀ кри́лома покрыва́ютъ ли́ца
своѧ̑, двѣма̀ же но́ги, и҆ двѣма̀ лѣта́юще,

SINGERS: **It is meet and right.**

The priest, bowing his head,
begins the Holy Anaphora:

For truly it is meet and right, fitting and proper to praise Thee, to hymn Thee, to bless Thee, to worship Thee, to glorify Thee, to give thanks unto Thee, the Fashioner of all creation, visible and invisible, the Treasury of eternal good things, the Source of life and immortality, the God and Master of all, who art hymned by the heavens and by the heavens of heavens and by all their powers, the sun and the moon, and the entire assembly of the stars, the earth, the sea and all that is therein, the heavenly Jerusalem, the assembly of the elect, the Church of the first-born written in heaven, the spirits of the righteous and the prophets, the souls of the martyrs and the apostles, the angels, archangels, thrones, principalities, authorities, dominions, and the dread powers, the many-eyed cherubim and the six-winged seraphim, who with two wings cover their

и҆ взыва́юще дрꙋ́гъ ко дрꙋ́гꙋ непреста́нными
оу҆сты̀, немо́лчными славослове́ньми:

Возглаше́нїе:

Побѣ́днꙋю пѣ́снь великолѣ́пныа твоеѧ̀
сла́вы свѣ́тлымъ гла́сомъ пою́ще, вопїю́ще,
славосло́ваще, взыва́юще и҆ глаго́люще:

Ли́къ: Ст҃ъ, ст҃ъ, ст҃ъ гдⷭ҇ь савао́ѳъ, и҆спо́лнь
нб҃о и҆ землѧ̀ сла́вы твоеѧ̀, ѡ҆са́нна въ
вы́шнихъ, блⷭ҇гослове́нъ грѧды́й во и҆́мѧ
гдⷭ҇не, ѡ҆са́нна въ вы́шнихъ.

Сщ҃е́нникъ знаменꙋ́етъ ст҃ы́ѧ
да́ры глаго́лѧ въ себѣ̀:

Ст҃ъ є҆сѝ ✠, цр҃ю̀ вѣкѡ́въ и҆ всѧ́кїѧ ст҃ы́ни
Гдⷭ҇ь и҆ пода́тель. ст҃ъ и҆ є҆диноро́дный
тво́й сн҃ъ ✠, гдⷭ҇ь на́шъ і҆и҃съ хрⷭ҇то́съ, и҆́мже
всѧ̀ сотвори́лъ є҆сѝ. ст҃ъ же и҆ дх҃ъ тво́й
прест҃ы́й ✠, и҆спытꙋ́ѧй всѧ́ческаѧ и҆ глꙋби́ны
твоѧ̀ бг҃а и҆ ѻ҆ц҃а̀.

И҆ приклони́въ главꙋ̀, мо́литсѧ та́йнѡ:

faces, with two their feet, and with two they fly, as they cry to one another with unceasing mouths, the and never-silent doxologies:

Exclamation:

Singing the triumphal hymn of Thy magnificent glory with a radiant voice, shouting, glorifying, crying, and saying:

SINGERS: Holy, holy, holy, Lord of Sabaoth, heaven and earth are full of Thy glory, hosanna in the highest, blessed is he who comes in the name of the Lord. Hosanna in the highest.

The priest signs the gifts,
saying within himself:

Holy art Thou ✠, O King of the ages, Lord and Giver of all holiness. Holy also is Thine only-begotten Son ✠, our Lord Jesus Christ, through whom Thou didst make all things, and holy also is Thine All-holy Spirit ✠, who searches all things and the depths of Thee, God and Father.

The priest, bowing, prays silently:

Ст҃ъ є҆сѝ, вседержи́телю всеси́льне, стра́шне, бл҃же, бл҃гоу́тро́бне, сострада́теленъ па́че ѡ҆ созда́нїи свое́мъ, сотвори́вый ѿ землѝ чл҃вѣ́ка по ѡ҆́бразꙋ своемꙋ̀ и҆ по подо́бїю, и҆ дарова́вый томꙋ̀ ра́йское наслажде́нїе, престꙋ́пивша же за́повѣдь твою̀, и҆ па́дша, того̀ не презрѣ́лъ є҆сѝ, нижѐ ѡ҆ста́вилъ є҆сѝ, бл҃же, но наказа́въ того̀ ꙗ҆́кѡ бл҃гоу́тро́бный ѻ҆ц҃ъ, призва́лъ є҆сѝ є҆го̀ зако́номъ, наꙋчи́лъ є҆сѝ того̀ прⷪ҇ро́ки, послѣ́ди же сама́гѡ є҆диноро́днаго твоегѡ̀ сн҃а, гдⷭ҇а на́шегѡ і҆и҃са хрⷭ҇та̀ посла́лъ є҆сѝ въ мі́ръ, ꙗ҆́кѡ да са́мъ прише́дъ тво́й ѡ҆бнови́тъ и҆ возста́витъ ѡ҆́бразъ, и҆́же сни́сшедъ съ небе́съ и҆ воплоти́вса ѿ дх҃а ст҃а и҆ мр҃і́н ст҃ы́а присноде́вы и҆ бц҃ы, спожи́ве же чл҃вѣ́кѡмъ, всѧ̑ оу҆стро́и ко спасе́нїю ро́да на́шегѡ.

Хотѧ́ще же во́льнꙋю и҆ животворѧ́щꙋю крⷭ҇то́мъ сме́рть, безгрѣ́шный за ны̀

Holy art Thou, Almighty, all-powerful, fear-some, good, and compassionate, who above all showest compassion for Thy creation, who didst make man out of the earth according to Thine image and likeness and didst grant unto him the delight of Paradise, but when he had transgressed Thy commandment and fallen away from it, Thou didst neither forsake him nor abandon him, O Good One, but didst instruct him as a compassionate Father. Thou didst call him through the Law, didst teach him though the prophets, but lastly Thou didst send into the world Thine only-begotten Son Himself, our Lord Jesus Christ, so that He, having come, might renew and restore Thine image. Having descended from the heavens and become incarnate of the Holy Spirit and the holy Ever-Virgin and Theotokos Mary, and having lived among men, He has disposed all things for the salvation of our race.

And when He was about to accept the voluntary and life-giving death on the Cross, the

гре́шныѧ, прїѧ́ти, въ но́щь, въ ню́же
преда́шесѧ, па́че же са́мъ себѐ преда́ше
за мі́рскі́й живо́тъ и҆ спасе́нїе:

Та́же, воста́въ и҆ взе́мъ ст҃ы́й хлѣ́бъ
зна́менꙋетъ є҆го̀ ✠, глаго́лѧ та́йнѡ:

Прїе́мъ хлѣ́бъ во ст҃ы́ѧ и҆ пречⷭ҇тыѧ и҆
непоро́чныѧ и҆ безсме́ртныѧ своѧ̀ рꙋ́ки,
воззрѣ́въ на не́бо и҆ показа́въ тебѣ̀ бг҃ꙋ
и҆ ѻ҆ц҃ꙋ̀, бл҃годари́въ, бл҃гослови́въ, ѡ҆ст҃и́въ,
преломи́въ, подадѐ ст҃ы́мъ и҆ бл҃же́ннымъ
свои҆мъ ᲂу҆ченикѡ́мъ и҆ а҆пⷭ҇лѡмъ, ре́къ:

Возглаше́нїе:
Прїими́те, ꙗ҆ди́те, сїѐ є҆́сть тѣ́ло моѐ,
є҆́же за вы̀ ломи́мое и҆ раздава́емое во
ѡ҆ставле́нїе грѣхѡ́въ.
Ли́къ: а҆ми́нь.

Та́же ст҃ꙋ́ю ча́шꙋ взе́мъ
и҆ зна́менꙋетъ ю҆ ✠ глаго́лѧ:
Та́кожде по ве́чери, прїе́мъ ча́шꙋ и҆ раствори́въ
ѿ вїна̀ и҆ воды̀, воззрѣ́въ на не́бо и҆
показа́въ тебѣ̀, бг҃ꙋ и҆ ѻ҆ц҃ꙋ̀, бл҃годари́въ,

Sinless one for us sinners, in the night in which He was given up, or rather gave Himself up for the life of the world and its salvation:

Then, rising, the priest takes the bread
and signs it ✠, saying quietly:

Taking bread into His holy, pure, blameless, and immortal hands, having looked up to heaven and shown it to Thee, the God and Father, having given thanks, blessed it, sanctified it, and broken it, He gave it to His holy and blessed disciples and apostles, saying:

Exclamation:

Take, eat: this is My Body which is broken and given for you for the remission of sins.
SINGERS: Amen.

Then the priest takes the chalice
and signs it ✠, saying:

Likewise, after supper, taking the cup and mixing it from wine and water, having looked up to heaven and shown it to Thee, the God

бл҃гословивъ, ѡ҆ст҃и́въ, и҆спо́лнивъ дх҃а ст҃а́гѡ, подадѐ ст҃ы̑мъ и҆ бл҃же́ннымъ свои̑мъ оу҆чени́кѡмъ и҆ а҆п҃лѡмъ, ре́къ:

Возгла́снѡ:

Пі́йте ѿ неѧ̀ всѝ: сїѧ̀ є҆́сть кро́вь моѧ̀ но́вагѡ завѣ́та, ꙗ҆́же за вы̀ и҆ за мнѡ́ги и҆злива́емаѧ и҆ раздава́емаѧ во ѡ҆ставле́нїе грѣхѡ́въ.

Ли́къ: А҆ми́нь.

Та́же, воста́вше глаго́летъ въ себѣ̀:

Сїѐ твори́те въ моѐ воспомина́нїе: є҆ли́жды бо а҆́ще ꙗ҆́сте хлѣ́бъ се́й и҆ ча́шꙋ сїю̀ пїе́те, сме́рть сн҃а чл҃вѣ́ческагѡ возвѣща́ете и҆ воскрⷭ҇нїе є҆гѡ̀ и҆сповѣ́дꙋете, до́ндеже прїи́детъ.

И҆ возглаша́ютъ дїа́кони вкꙋ́пѣ: Вѣ́рꙋемъ и҆ и҆сповѣ́дꙋемъ.

Пѣвцы̀ ѿвѣща́ютъ: Сме́рть твою̀, гдⷭ҇и, возвѣща́емъ, и҆ воскрⷭ҇нїе твоѐ и҆сповѣ́дꙋемъ.

and Father, having given thanks, blessed it, sanctified it, and filled it with the Holy Spirit, He gave it to His holy and blessed disciples and apostles, saying:

Exclamation:

Drink of it, all of you: this is My Blood of the New Covenant, which is shed and given for you and for many for the remission of sins! SINGERS: Amen.

Then, rising, the priest says within himself:

Do this in remembrance of Me, for as often as ye eat this bread and drink this cup, ye proclaim the death of the Son of man, and confess His Resurrection, until He comes.

And the deacons exclaim together:
We believe and confess!

The singers respond:
We proclaim Thy death, O Lord, and we confess Thy resurrection!

Сщ҃е́нникъ же зна́менꙋетъ ѻ҆бо́ѧ ст҃ы́ѧ да́ры ✠ и҆ приклони́въ главꙋ̀ глаго́летъ:

Помина́юще оу҆̀бѡ и҆ мы̀, грѣ́шнїи, животворѧ́щїѧ є҆гѡ̀ стра́сти и҆ спаси́тельный крⷭ҇тъ и҆ сме́рть и҆ погребе́нїе, и҆ тридне́вное и҆зъ ме́ртвыхъ воскрⷭ҇нїе и҆ на небеса̀ восхожде́нїе и҆ ѡ҆деснꙋ́ю тебѣ̀, бг҃а и҆ ѻ҆ц҃а̀, сѣдѣ́нїе, и҆ второ́е и҆ сла́вное и҆ стра́шное є҆гѡ̀ прише́ствїе, є҆гда̀ прїи́детъ со сла́вою сꙋди́ти живы́мъ и҆ ме́ртвымъ, є҆гда̀ хо́щетъ возда́ти коемꙋ́ждо по дѣлѡ́мъ є҆гѡ̀: пощади́ на́съ, гдⷭ҇и бж҃е на́шъ (г҃-жды), наипа́че же по бл҃гоꙋтро́бїю є҆гѡ̀ прино́симъ тѝ, влⷣко, стра́шнꙋю сїю̀ и҆ безкро́внꙋю же́ртвꙋ, молѧ́щесѧ, ꙗ҆́кѡ да не по грѣхѡ́мъ на́шимъ сотвори́ши съ на́ми, ниже́ по беззако́нїемъ на́шимъ возда́си на́мъ, но по твоемꙋ̀ снисхожде́нїю и҆ неизрече́нномꙋ чл҃вѣколю́бїю презрѣ́въ и҆ потреби́въ є҆́же на на́съ рꙋкописа́нїе твои́хъ рабѡ́въ, да́рꙋй на́мъ небе́снаѧ и҆ вѣ́чнаѧ твоѧ̀ дарова́нїѧ, ꙗ҆̀же ѻ҆́ко не ви́дѣ, и҆ оу҆́хо не слы́ша, и҆ на

Then, signing both the holy gifts ✠ and
bowing his head, the priest says:

We, sinners, also, remembering His life-giving Passion and the saving Cross,
death, burial, and the third-day Resurrection
from the dead, the ascension into the heavens and the sitting at the right hand of Thee,
God and Father, and His second, glorious,
and dread Coming, when He shall come with
glory to judge the living and the dead, when He
shall render to each according to his works—
Spare us, O Lord our God! (three times)—or
rather in accordance with His compassion,
we offer unto Thee, O Master, this dread and
bloodless sacrifice, praying that Thou mightest not deal with us according to our sins, nor
reward us according to our transgressions,
but in Thy forbearance and ineffable love for
mankind having overlooked and expunged
the handwriting which is against us, Thy suppliants, Thou mayest grant us Thy heavenly
and eternal gifts, which eye hath not seen nor

се́рдце чл҃вѣ́кꙋ не взы́де, ꙗ҆́же ѹ҆готова́лъ
е҆сѝ, бж҃е, лю́бѧцимъ тѧ̀, и҆ да не менѐ
ра́ди и҆ мои́хъ ра́ди грѣхѡ́въ ѿри́неши лю́ди
своѧ̀, чл҃вѣколю́бче гд҃и, гд҃и си́лъ, нижѐ да
возврацꙋ́сѧ смире́нъ и҆ посрамле́нъ:

Та́же возглаша́етъ и҆лѝ
пое́тъ:

Лю́дїе бо твои̑ и҆ цр҃ковь твоѧ̀ мо́лѧтъ
тѧ̀.

Пѣвцы̀ же ѿвѣща́ютъ:

Поми́лꙋй на́съ, гд҃и бж҃е, ѻ҆́че
вседержи́телю.

И҆ па́ки пое́тъ сц҃е́нникъ съ сослꙋжа́цими
то́жде: Лю́дїе бо твои̑ и҆ цр҃ковь твоѧ̀:
и҆ прѡ́чаѧ, и҆ па́ки ѿвѣща́ютъ пѣвцы̀:
Поми́лꙋй на́съ: и҆ прѡ́чаѧ. та́кѡ да
три́жды пое́тъ сц҃е́нникъ съ сослꙋжа́цими
и҆ три́жды ѿвѣща́ютъ е҆мꙋ̀ пѣвцы̀. Тре́тїе
же пѣвцы̀ пою́тъ вельмѝ кѡ́снѡ.

ear heard, neither hath entered into the heart of man what Thou hast prepared, O God, for those who love Thee; and mayest Thou not forsake Thy people on account of me and on account of my sins, O Lord who lovest mankind, Thou Lord of hosts, and may I not be turned away, humbled and ashamed,

And he exclaims or sings:

For Thy people and Thy Church supplicate Thee:

And the singers respond:

Have mercy on us, O Lord God, Father almighty!

And again the priest sings with the concelebrants the same: For Thy people and Thy Church . . . , and the rest, and the singers respond again: Have mercy on us . . . , and the rest. Thus, the priest, together with the concelebrants, sings it thrice, and the singers respond to him thrice. But the third time, the singers sing very slowly.

Та́же воста́въ мо́литса сщ҃е́нникъ въ себѣ̀:

Помилꙋ́й на́съ, бж҃е на́шъ, ѻ҆́че вседер_жи́телю. Помилꙋ́й на́съ, бж҃е спа́се на́шъ. Помилꙋ́й на́съ, бж҃е, по вели́цѣй ми́лости твое́й, и҆ послѝ на ны̀ и҆ на предлежа́щїѧ ст҃ы́ѧ да́ры сїѧ̀ дх҃а твоегѡ̀ прест҃а́гѡ:

И҆ приклони́ь главꙋ̀,
мо́литса та́йнѡ:

Гд҃а и҆ животворѧ́щаго, сопресто́льнаго тебѣ̀, бг҃ꙋ и҆ ѻ҆ц҃ꙋ, и҆ є҆диноро́дномꙋ твоемꙋ̀ сн҃ꙋ, и҆ соца́рствꙋема, є҆диносꙋ́щна же и҆ соприсносꙋ́щна, глаго́лавшаго въ зако́нѣ и҆ прⷬ҇ро́кахъ и҆ въ но́вѣмъ твое́мъ завѣ́тѣ, соше́дшаго въ ви́дѣ голꙋби́нѣ на гд҃а на́шего і҆и҃са хрⷭ҇та̀ на і҆ѻрда́нстѣй рѣцѣ̀ и҆ пребы́вша на не́мъ, соше́дшаго на ст҃ы́ѧ твоѧ̀ а҆п҃лы въ видѣ́нїи ѻ҆́гненныхъ а҆зы́къ, въ го́рницѣ ст҃а́гѡ и҆ сла́внагѡ сїѡ́на въ де́нь ст҃ы́ѧ патидеса́тницы:

И҆ воста́въ глаго́летъ въ себѣ̀:

Са́маго дх҃а твоегѡ̀ прест҃а́гѡ ниспосли́, влⷣко,

Then, rising, the priest prays within himself:

Have mercy on us, our God, Father almighty. Have mercy on us, O God our Saviour. Have mercy on us, O God, according to thy great mercy, and send upon us and upon these holy gifts that are set forth Thine All-holy Spirit:

And, bowing down, he says:

The Lord and Giver of life, co-enthroned with Thee, God and Father, and with Thine only-begotten Son, co-reigning, consubstantial, and co-eternal, who spake in the Law and the prophets and in thy New Covenant, who descended in the form of a dove upon our Lord Jesus Christ in the river Jordan and abode upon Him, who descended upon Thy holy Apostles in the form of fiery tongues in the upper room of holy and glorious Sion on the day of Holy Pentecost:

And, rising, he says:

Thy same All-holy Spirit do Thou send down,

на ны̀ и҆ на предлежа́щїѧ да́ры сїѧ̀, ꙗ҆́кѡ да посѣти́въ ст҃ы́мъ и҆ бл҃ги́мъ и҆ сла́внымъ є҆гѡ̀ прише́ствїемъ, ѡ҆сти́тъ и҆ сотвори́тъ оу҆́бо хлѣ́бъ се́й тѣ́ло ст҃о́е хр҃то́во.

И҆ зна́менꙋетъ ✠ сщ҃е́нникъ ст҃ы́й хлѣ́бъ.

Дїа́кони: а҆ми́нь.

Сщ҃е́нникъ: И҆ ча́шꙋ сїю̀ кро́вь честнꙋ́ю хр҃то́вꙋ.

И҆ зна́менꙋетъ ✠ ст҃ꙋ́ю ча́шꙋ.

Дїа́кони: а҆ми́нь.

Та́же мо́литсѧ сщ҃е́нникъ:

Ꙗ҆́кѡ да бꙋ́дꙋтъ всѣ́мъ и҆́же ѿ ни́хъ причаща́ющимсѧ во ѡ҆ставле́нїе грѣхѡ́въ и҆ въ жи́знь вѣ́чнꙋю, во ѡ҆чище́нїе дꙋ́шъ и҆ тѣле́съ, во плодоноше́нїе бл҃ги́хъ дѣ́лъ, во оу҆твержде́нїе ст҃ы́ѧ твоеѧ̀ собо́рныѧ и҆ а҆пльскі́ѧ цр҃кве, ю҆́же ѡ҆снова́лъ є҆сѝ на ка́мени вѣ́ры, ꙗ҆́кѡ и҆ врата̀ а҆́довы не ѡ҆долѣ́ютъ є҆́й, и҆збавлѧ́ѧ ю҆̀ ѿ всѧ́кїѧ є҆́реси и҆ ѿ соблазнѡ́въ дѣ́лающихъ беззако́нїе

O Master, upon us and upon these holy gifts set forth, that having come by His holy, good, and glorious presence, He may sanctify and make this bread the holy Body of Christ.

And the priest signs ✠ the holy Bread.
DEACONS: Amen.
PRIEST: And this cup the precious Blood of Christ.

And he signs ✠ the holy Chalice.
DEACONS: Amen.

Then the priest prays:

That they may be to all who partake of them for the remission of sins and for life eternal; for the sanctification of souls and bodies, for the fruition of good works, for the strengthening of Thy holy, catholic, and apostolic Church, which Thou didst establish upon the rock of faith, so that the gates of hell shall not prevail against her, delivering her from every heresy and scandal of those who work iniquity and

и̑ ѿ всѣ́хъ воста́вшихъ и̑ востаю́щихъ на
вра́гъ, да́же до сконча́нїѧ вѣ́ка.

И̑ зна́менꙋетъ ст҃ы́й хлѣ́бъ ✠ и̑ ст҃ы́й
поти́ръ ✠.

И̑ ѿвѣща́ютъ вси́ сꙋ́щыѧ во ст҃и́лище:
а̑ми́нь.

Та́же сщ҃е́нникъ, приклони́въ главꙋ̀,
мо́литсѧ, пѣвцы̀ же припѣва́ютъ
многа́жды ко́снѡ:
Помѧни́, гд҃и бж҃е на́шъ.

Сщ҃е́нникъ:

Прино́симъ тѝ, влⷣко и̑ ѡ ст҃ы́хъ
твои́хъ мѣ́стѣхъ, ꙗ҃́же просла́вилъ
є̑сѝ бг҃оѧвле́нїемъ хрⷭта̀ твоегѡ̀ и̑ наи́тїемъ
прест҃а́гѡ твоегѡ̀ дх҃а, пе́рвѣе бо ѡ ст҃ѣ́мъ
и̑ сла́внѣмъ сїѡ́нѣ, ма́тери всѣ́хъ цр҃кве́й,
и̑ ѡ и̑̀же по все́й вселе́ннѣй ст҃ѣ́й твое́й
собо́рнѣй и̑ а̑пⷭльстѣ́й цр҃кви, бога́тнѣ и̑
ны́нѣ да́ры прест҃а́гѡ твоегѡ̀ дх҃а пода́ждь
є̑́й, влⷣко.

Помѧни́, гд҃и, и̑ и̑̀же въ не́й ст҃ы́хъ

from the enemies that arose and now rise up against her, even to the end of the age.

And he signs the holy Bread ✠ and the holy Chalice ✠.

Then all the clergy in the sanctuary respond:
Amen.

Then the priest bows his head and prays, while the singers chant slowly and many times:
Remember, O Lord our God.

Priest:

We make this offering unto Thee, Master, also for Thy holy places, which Thou didst glorify by the theophany of Thy Christ and by the visitation of Thine All-holy Spirit; first of all, for holy and glorious Sion, mother of all the Churches, and for thy holy, catholic, and apostolic Church throughout the world: do Thou, O Master, abundantly grant to her even now the gifts of Thine All-holy Spirit.

Remember also, O Lord, our holy fathers

ѻ҆те́цъ на́шихъ и҆ є҆пи́скопѡвъ, и҆̀же повсю́дꙋ во все́й вселе́ннѣй правосла́внѡ пра́вѡ пра́вꙗщихъ сло́во твоеѧ̀ и҆́стины.

Возглаше́нїе:

Въ пе́рвыхъ помѧнѝ, гд҃и, ст҃а́го ѻ҆тца̀ на́шегѡ, а҆рхїепкопа (и҆лѝ митрополі́та) и҆м҃къ, ве́сь при́четъ и҆ сщ҃е́нство є҆гѡ̀, ста́рость є҆мꙋ̀ честнꙋ́ю да́рꙋй, долголѣ́тна є҆гѡ̀ сохранѝ, пасꙋ́ща лю́ди твоѧ̀ во вса́комъ бл҃гоче́стїи и҆ чистотѣ̀.

Ли́къ: Помѧнѝ, гд҃и бж҃е на́шъ.

Сщ҃е́нникъ же мо́лится:

Помѧнѝ, гд҃и, и҆ є҆́же здѐ честно́е прес_ вꙋ́терство, и҆ є҆́же повсю́дꙋ во хр҃тѣ̀ дїа́конство, про́чее вса́кое слꙋже́нїе, ве́сь цр҃ко́вный чи́нъ и҆ є҆́же во хр҃тѣ̀ бра́тство на́ше и҆ вса̀ хр҃толюби́выꙗ лю́ди.

Помѧнѝ, гд҃и, и҆̀же съ на́ми предстоѧ́щыꙗ сщ҃е́нники, въ се́й ст҃ый ча́съ пре́дъ ст҃ы́мъ твои́мъ же́ртвенникомъ во приноше́нїе ст҃ы́ꙗ и҆ безкро́вныꙗ твоеѧ̀ же́ртвы, и҆ да́ждь и҆̀мъ

and bishops which are in her, those who everywhere, in all the world rightly, in the Orthodox manner, divide the word of Thy truth.

Exclamation:

Among the first, remember, O Lord, our holy father, Archbishop [or: Metropolitan] N., all his clergy and sacred order, grant him an honorable old age, preserve him for many years, shepherding thy people in all piety and holiness.

SINGERS: Remember, O Lord our God.

And the priest prays:

Remember, O Lord, the honorable presbytery and the diaconate in Christ here and everywhere, every other ministry, every order of the Church and our brotherhood in Christ and all Christ-loving people.

Remember, O Lord, the priests who concelebrate with us at the offering of Thy holy and bloodless sacrifice in this holy hour

и̑ на́мх сло́во во ѿверзе́нїе ꙋстх на́шихх во
сла́вꙋ и̑ хвалꙋ прест҃а́гѡ и̑мени твоегѡ̀.

Помѧнѝ, гд҃и, по мно́жествꙋ ми́лости
твоеѧ̀ и̑ щедро́тх твои́хх и̑ менѐ, смире́ннагѡ
и̑ грѣ́шнагѡ и̑ недосто́йнагѡ раба̀ твоегѡ̀,
и̑ посѣти́ мѧ ми́лостїю и̑ щедро́тами, и̑
и̑зба́ви и̑ непови́нна сотворѝ ѿ гонѧ́щихх
мѧ, гд҃и, гд҃и си́лх, и̑ поне́же ꙋмно́жисѧ во
мнѣ̀ грѣ́хх, да преизбы́точествꙋетх твоѧ̀
бл҃года́ть.

Помѧнѝ, гд҃и, и̑же ст҃ы́й тво́й жр҃т-
венникх ѡ̑крꙋжа́ющыѧ дїа́коны, и̑ да́рꙋй
и̑мх житїѐ непоро́чно, несквернꙋ и̑хх слꙋ́жбꙋ
сохранѝ и̑ степе́ни бл҃га̑ и̑мх снабдѝ.

Помѧнѝ, гд҃и, ст҃ы́й бг҃а на́шегѡ гра́дх,
и̑ цр҃твꙋющїй гра́дх, и̑ гра́дх се́й (и̑ли: ст҃ꙋ́ю
ѡ̑би́тель сїю̀), и̑ всѧ́кїй гра́дх и̑ странꙋ̀,
и̑ и̑же правосла́вною вѣ́рою и̑ бл҃гоче́стїемх
живꙋ́щихх вх ни́хх, ми́рх и̑ ꙋтвержде́нїе
и̑хх.

Помѧнѝ, гд҃и, бг҃охрани́мꙋю странꙋ̀ сїю̀,
прави́телей и̑ во́инство и̑хх, ꙋстро́й и̑хх

before Thy holy altar; and give them and us a word to open our mouths to the glory and praise of Thine All-holy Name.,

Remember, O Lord, according to the multitude of Thy mercy and Thy compassion, me also, Thy humble, sinful, and unworthy servant, and visit me in mercy and compassion, deliver me unharmed from those who persecute me, O Lord, Thou Lord of hosts, and because sin increased in me, may Thy grace abound in me also.

Remember, O Lord, the deacons who surround Thy holy altar, and grant them a life without blemish, preserve their diaconate spotless, and obtain for them good degrees.

Remember, O Lord, the holy city of our God, the royal city, this city [or this holy monastery], and every city and countryside and the peace and safety of those who in Orthodox faith and piety dwell therein.

Remember, O Lord, this God-preserved land, its rulers and armed forces; set in order

совѣ́ты, ꙗ҆́кѡ да и҆ мы̀ ти́хое и҆ безмо́лвное
житїѐ поживе́мъ во вса́комъ бл҃гоче́стїи и҆
чистотѣ̀.

Помѧнѝ, гд҃и, пла́вающихъ, пꙋте_
ше́ствꙋющихъ, стра́нничествꙋющихъ
хрⷭ҇тїа́нъ, во ѹ҆́захъ и҆ темни́цахъ, и҆ въ
плѣне́нїи и҆ въ заточе́нїи, и҆ въ рꙋда́хъ и҆
мꙋ́кахъ, и҆ въ го́рькихъ рабо́тахъ сꙋ́щихъ
ѻ҆ц҃ъ и҆ бра́тїй на́шихъ, ми́рное возвраще́нїе
коегѡ́ждо ѿ ни́хъ во своѧ̑ сѝ.

Помѧнѝ, гд҃и, и҆̀же въ ста́рости и҆ въ
не́мощи сꙋ́щихъ, недꙋ́гꙋющихъ, стра́ж_
дꙋщихъ и҆ и҆̀же ѿ дꙋ́хѡвъ нечи́стыхъ
стꙋжа́емыхъ, ѿ тебѐ, бг҃а, ско́рое и҆сцѣле́нїе
и҆ спасе́нїе и҆́хъ.

Помѧнѝ, гд҃и, вса́кꙋю дꙋ́шꙋ хрⷭ҇тїа́нскꙋю,
скорбѧ́щꙋю и҆ ѡ҆би́димꙋю, ми́лости и҆
по́мощи ѿ тебѐ, бг҃а, требꙋ́ющꙋю, и҆
ѡ҆браще́нїе заблꙋ́ждшихъ.

Помѧнѝ, гд҃и, и҆̀же въ дѣ́вствѣ и҆ бл҃го_
че́стїи и҆ по́стничествѣ пребыва́ющихъ, и҆
и҆̀же въ гора́хъ и҆ въ верте́пѣхъ и҆ въ про́пастехъ

their counsels, that we also may lead a quiet and peaceful life in all godliness and sanctity.

Remember, O Lord, the Christians who sail and travel, who sojourn in foreign lands, those of our fathers and brethren who are in chains and in prisons, in captivity and in exile, in mines and tortures and bitter slavery, and the peaceful return of each one of them into their homes.

Remember, O Lord, those who are in old age and infirmity, the sick, the afflicted, and those assailed by unclean spirits, their speedy recovery and salvation from Thee, our God.

Remember, O Lord, every Christian soul, afflicted and heavy laden, entreating mercy and help from Thee, O God, and the return of those who are deceived.

Remember, O Lord, those who abide in virginity, piety, and asceticism, and our venerable fathers and brethren who struggle on mountains and in caves and pits of the earth, and every Orthodox congregation in every

земны́хъ подвиза́ющихсѧ ѻ҆ц҃ъ и҆ бра́тїй на́шихъ и҆ и҆́же по разли́чнымъ мѣстѡ́мъ правосла́вныхъ собра́нїѧ, и҆ и҆́же здѣ̀ во хрⷭ҇тѣ̀ собра́нїе на́ше.

Помѧнѝ, гдⷭ҇и, трꙋжда́ющихсѧ и҆ слꙋжа́щихъ на́мъ ѻ҆ц҃ъ же и҆ бра́тїй на́шихъ и҆́мене твоегѡ̀ ра́ди ст҃а́гѡ. Помѧнѝ, гдⷭ҇и, всѣ́хъ во бл҃го, всѣ́хъ поми́лꙋй, влⷣко, всѣ́хъ на́съ примирѝ, оу҆мирѝ мно́жество люде́й твои́хъ, разорѝ собла́зны, оу҆празднѝ бра́ни, оу҆толѝ раздра́нїѧ церкѡ́внаѧ, є҆рети́ческаѧ воста́нїѧ ско́рѡ разрꙋшѝ, низложѝ шата́нїе ꙗ҆зы́кѡвъ, возвы́си ро́гъ хрⷭ҇тїа́нскїй, тво́й ми́ръ и҆ твою̀ любо́вь да́рꙋй на́мъ, бж҃е спа́се на́шъ, оу҆пова́нїе всѣ́хъ концє́въ землѝ.

Помѧнѝ, гдⷭ҇и, бл҃горастворе́нїе возд꙼ꙋ́хѡвъ, дождѝ ми́рныѧ, рѡ́сы бл҃гі́ѧ, плодѡ́въ и҆з҆оби́лїе, соверше́нное плодо_ро́дїе, и҆ вѣне́цъ лѣ́та бл҃гости твоеѧ̀, ѻ҆́чи бо всѣ́хъ на тѧ̀ оу҆пова́ютъ и҆ ты̀ да́еши пи́щꙋ и҆̀мъ во бл҃говре́менїи, ѿверза́еши ты̀

place, and this our congregation in Christ in this place.

Remember, O Lord, our fathers and brethren who toil and serve us for the sake of Thy holy name. Remember, O Lord, everyone for their benefit: O Master, have mercy on all; be reconciled with us all, give peace to the multitudes of Thy people, disperse scandals, abolish wars, make divisions of the churches to cease, speedily destroy the uprisings of heresies, overthrow the insolence of the nations, raise up the horn of Christians, grant us Thy peace and Thy love, O God our Saviour, Thou hope of all the ends of the earth.

Remember, O Lord, seasonable weather, peaceful rains, good dews, abundance of fruits, a full harvest, and the crown of the year of Thy goodness: for the eyes of all hope on Thee and Thou givest them their food in due season, Thou openest Thy hand and fillest every living being with good pleasure.

Remember, O Lord, those who bear fruit

рꙋ́кꙋ твою̀ и̑ и̑сполнѧ́еши всѧ́ко живо́тно
бл҃говоле́нїа.

Помѧнѝ, гдⷭ҇и, плодоносѧ́щихъ и̑
плодоноси́вшихъ во ст҃ы́хъ твои́хъ
бж҃їихъ цр҃квахъ, поминаю̀щихъ ѹ̑бѡ́гїа,
и̑ запове́давшихъ на́мъ недосто́йнымъ
помина́ти и̑хъ въ мл҃твахъ.

Є̑щѐ помѧнꙋ́ти сподо́би, гдⷭ҇и, и̑ и̑̀же
приноше́нїа принѐ́сшихъ въ дне́шнїй де́нь
во ст҃ы́й тво́й же́ртвенникъ, и̑ ѡ̑ ни́хже
кі́йждо принесѐ, и̑лѝ въ помышле́нїи
и̑́мать, и̑ ны́нѣ тебѣ̀ прочте́нныѧ.

Здѣ̀ помина́етъ сщ҃е́нникъ и̑̀хже хо́щетъ
помѧнꙋ́ти живы́хъ, глаго́лѧ въ себѣ̀:
Помѧнѝ, гдⷭ҇и, и̑ роди́тели на́ша и̑ сро́дники
и̑ дрꙋ́ги и̑́мⷦ҇ъ.

И̑ бл҃гослови́вшꙋ сщ҃е́нникꙋ,
дїа́конъ возглаша́етъ:

Ѡ̑спасе́нїи, ми́рѣ, ми́лости, любвѝ,
сохране́нїи и̑ застꙋпле́нїи ст҃ѣ́йшихъ
патрїа́рхѡвъ правосла́вныхъ, и̑ патрїа́рха

and those who have borne fruit in Thy holy
churches of God, those who remember the
poor and those who have commanded us
unworthy ones to remember them in our
prayers.

Again, deign also to remember, O Lord,
those who have brought these offerings on
this day to Thy holy altar and those for whom
each has brought them or whom they have in
mind and those whose names have now been
read.

Here the priest commemorates
whomever he wishes from among the living,
saying within himself:

Remember, Lord, also our parents, kinsmen,
and friends N. and N.

And after the priest blesses the deacon,
the deacon begins to say thus aloud:

For the salvation, peace, mercy, love, protection and help of the most holy Orthodox patriarchs, and of our holy Patriarch N.,

на́шегѡ и҆м҃къ и҆ а҆рхїепи́скопа (и҆ли́:
митрополі́та) на́шегѡ и҆м҃къ, и҆ про́чихъ
ст҃ы́хъ Ѻ҆тє́цъ и҆ є҆пи́скопѡвъ, и҆́же во все́й
вселе́ннѣй правосла́внѡ пра́вѡ пра́вѧщихъ
сло́во и҆́стины, всѧ́кїй чи́нъ цр҃ко́вный и҆ ѡ҆
прави́телехъ и҆ всѣ́хъ во вла́сти сꙋ́щихъ, да
ти́хое и҆ безмо́лвное житїѐ поживе́мъ во
всѧ́комъ бл҃гоче́стїи и҆ чистотѣ̀.

Ли́къ: Помѧнѝ, гд҃и бж҃е на́шъ.

Дїа́конъ: Є҆щѐ ѡ҆ пресвѵ́терахъ, дїа́конехъ,
ѵ҆подїа́конехъ, чтецє́хъ, пѣвцє́хъ, мона́-
сехъ, приснодѣ́вахъ, вдови́цахъ, си́рыхъ,
воздє́ржницехъ и҆ въ сщ҃е́нномъ бра́цѣ
пребыва́ющихъ и҆ хр҃толюби́выхъ лю́дехъ.

Ли́къ: Помѧнѝ, гд҃и бж҃е на́шъ.

Глаго́лемꙋ же семꙋ̀, мо́литсѧ сщ҃е́нникъ:

Си́хъ всѣ́хъ помѧнѝ, гд҃и, и҆́хже помѧнꙋ́хомъ
и҆ и҆́хже не помѧнꙋ́хомъ правосла́вныхъ,
возда́ждь и҆̀мъ вмѣ́стѡ земны́хъ нбⷭ҇наѧ,
вмѣ́стѡ тлѣ́нныхъ нетлѣ́ннаѧ, вмѣ́стѡ

and our Archbishop [or Metropolitan] N., and of other holy fathers and bishops who in all the world in the Orthodox manner rightly divide the word of the truth, for every order of the Orthodox church, and for the rulers and all who are in authority, that we may lead a quiet and peaceful life in all godliness and sanctity.

SINGERS: Remember, O Lord our God.

DEACON: Again for the presbyters, deacons, subdeacons, readers, singers, monastics, virgins, widows, orphans, ascetics, and for those who lead their life in sacred marriage, and the Christ-loving people.

SINGERS: Remember, O Lord our God.

While this is said, the priest prays:

Remember, O Lord, all those whom we have remembered and those of the Orthodox whom we have not remembered; grant them heavenly things for earthly, incorruptible things for corruptible, things eternal for

вре́менныхъ в꙼ѣ́чнаѧ, по ѡ҆б꙼ѣтова́нїю хр҇та̀ твоегѡ̀.

Поне́же бо живота̀ и҆ сме́рти ѻ҆́бласть и҆́маши, е҆щѐ помѧнꙋ́ти сподо́би, гд҇и, и҆̀же ѿ в꙼ѣ́ка теб꙼ѣ̀ бл҃гоꙋгоди́вшїѧ въ ро́дъ и҆ ро́дъ ст҃ы́ѧ ѻ҆тцы̀, патрїа́рхи, пр҇ро́цы, а҆п҇ли, мч҇еницы, и҆спов꙼ѣ́дницы, оу҆чи́телїе, преподо́бныѧ и҆ всѧ́кїй дꙋ́хъ пра́ведный въ в꙼ѣ́р꙼ѣ хр҇та̀ твоегѡ̀ скончавшї́йсѧ.

Помѧнѝ, гд҇и, а҆рха́гг҃льскїй гла́съ глаго́лющъ: ра́дꙋйсѧ, бл҃года́тнаѧ, гд҇ь съ тобо́ю, бл҃гослове́на ты̀ въ жена́хъ и҆ бл҃гослове́нъ пло́дъ чре́ва твоегѡ̀, досто-бл҃же́ннаѧ, ꙗ҆́кѡ сп҃са роди́ла е҆сѝ дꙋ́шъ на́шихъ.

Поклонѧ́ѧсѧ,
сщ҃е́нникъ возглаша́етъ:

И҆зрѧ́днѡ ѡ҆ прест҃꙼ѣ́й, пречⷭ҇т꙼ѣ́й, пребл҃гослове́нн꙼ѣй вл҃чц꙼ѣ на́шей бц҃꙼ѣ и҆ приснод꙼ѣ́в꙼ѣ мр҃і́и.

things temporal, according to the promise of Thy Christ.

As Thou hast power over life and death, again deign to remember, O Lord, also those who from the ages have been well-pleasing unto Thee from generation unto generation: the holy fathers, patriarchs, prophets, apostles, martyrs, confessors, teachers, ascetics, and every righteous spirit made perfect in the faith of Thy Christ.

Remember, O Lord, the voice of the archangel, saying: "Rejoice, O full of grace, the Lord is with thee! Blessed art thou among women, and blessed is the Fruit of thy womb, thou worthy of blessing, for thou hast borne the Saviour of our souls."

Bowing, the priest says the exclamation:

Especially our most holy, most pure, most blessed Lady Theotokos and Ever-Virgin Mary.

И҆ па́ки глю́тъ пѣвцы̀, ꙗ҆́кѡже пе́рвѣе:
Помѧнѝ, гдⷭ҇и бж҃е на́шъ.

Сщ҃е́нникъ же мо́лится та́йнѡ:

Ста́гѡ і҆ѡа́нна прⷪ҇ро́ка, прⷣте́чи и҆ крⷭ҇ти́телѧ,
ст҃ы́хъ а҆пⷭ҇лъ петра̀, па́ѵла, а҆ндре́а, і҆а́кѡва,
і҆ѡа́нна, фїлі́ппа, варѳоломе́а, ѳѡмы̀,
матѳе́а, і҆а́кѡва, сѵ́мѡна, і҆ꙋ́дꙋ, матѳі́а,
ма́рка и҆ лꙋкѝ є҆ѵⷢ҇гелі́стѡвъ, ст҃ы́хъ
прⷪ҇ро́кѡвъ, патрїа́рхѡвъ и҆ пра́ведникъ, ста́гѡ
стефа́на, а҆рхїдїа́кона и҆ первомⷱ҇ника, ст҃ы́хъ
мⷱ҇никѡвъ и҆ и҆сповѣ́дникѡвъ, и҆́же за хрⷭ҇та̀,
и҆́стиннагѡ бг҃а на́шегѡ, пострада́вшихъ и҆
и҆сповѣ́давшихъ до́брое и҆сповѣ́данїе, и҆
ст҃ы́хъ мⷧ҇а́нецъ, и҆збїе́нныхъ ѿ и҆́рода царѧ̀.

Помѧнѝ, гдⷭ҇и, ст҃ы́хъ мⷱ҇никѡвъ
проко́пїа, ѳео́дѡра, кѵ́ра, і҆ѡа́нна, гео́ргїа,
леѡ́нтїа, се́ргїа, ва́кха, космы̀, дамїа́на,
савїнїа́на, па́ѵла, вавꙋ́лꙋ, а҆гаѳа́нгела,
є҆ѵстра́тїа и҆ и҆̀же съ ни́мъ пострада́вшихъ,
ст҃ы́хъ четы́редесѧть мⷱ҇ченикѡвъ, ст҃ы́ѧ
первомꙋ́ченицы ѳе́клы, ст҃ы́хъ же́нъ
мѷроно́сицъ, и҆ мⷱ҇ченицъ татїа́ны,

And the singers say, as before:
Remember, O Lord our God.

The priest prays:

The holy Prophet, Forerunner and Baptist John, the holy apostles Peter, Paul, Andrew, James, John, Philip, Bartholomew, Thomas, Matthew, James, Simon, Jude, Matthias, Mark and Luke, the evangelists; the holy prophets, patriarchs, and righteous, the first deacon and protomartyr Stephen, the holy martyrs and confessors who bore witness on account of Christ the true God, and who professed the good confession; and the holy infants murdered by Herod the king.

Remember, O Lord, the holy martyrs Procopius, Theodore, Cyrus and John, George, Leontius, Sergius and Bacchus, Cosmas and Damian, Sabinian, Paul, Babylas, Agathangelus, Eustratius and those who suffered with him, the holy Forty Martyrs, the holy first woman martyr Thecla, the holy myrrhbearing women and the women martyrs Tatiana,

феврѡ́ніи, а҆наста́сіи, е҆ѵфи́міи, сѡфі́и, варва́ры, і҆ꙋліа́ніи, і҆ри́ны, наде́жды, вѣ́ры, любвѐ.

Помѧнѝ, гд҃и, ст҃ы́хъ ѻ҆т҃е́цъ на́шихъ и҆ а҆рхїепі́скопѡвъ и҆́же ѿ ст҃а́гѡ і҆а́кѡва а҆п҃ла и҆ бра́та гд҃нѧ да́же до сегѡ̀ днѐ правосла́внѡ а҆рхїепі́скопствовавшихъ ст҃ꙋ́ю цр҃ковь бг҃а на́шегѡ во ст҃ѣ́мъ гра́дѣ твое́мъ.

Помѧнѝ, гд҃и, ст҃ы́хъ ѻ҆т҃е́цъ на́шихъ и҆ оу҆чи́телей кли́мента, тїмѡ̈ѳе́а, і҆гна́тїа, дїонѵ́сіа, і҆рине́а, петра̀, григо́ріа, а҆леѯа́ндра, е҆ѵста́ѳіа, а҆ѳана́сіа, васі́ліа, григо́ріа, григо́ріа, а҆мвро́сіа, а҆мфіло́хїа, ливе́рїа, дама́сіа, і҆ѡа́нна, е҆пїфа́нїа, ѳео́фила, келести́на, а҆ѵгꙋсти́на, кѷрі́лла, льва̀, про́кла, проте́рїа, фели́ѯа, ѻ҆рмі́сда, е҆ѵло́гіа, марти́на, а҆га́ѳѡна, сѡфро́нїа.

Помѧнѝ, гд҃и, ст҃ы́хъ вели́кихъ и҆ вселе́нскихъ се́дмь собо́рѡвъ и҆ про́чїа ст҃ы́ѧ собо́ры и҆ е҆пі́скопы и҆́же по все́й вселе́ннѣй правосла́внѡ и҆ пра́вѡ и҆справлѧ́ющихъ сло́во и҆́стины.

Помѧнѝ, гд҃и, ст҃ы́хъ преподо́бныхъ

Febronia, Anastasia, Euphemia, Sophia, Barbara, Juliana, Irene, Hope, Faith, and Love.

Remember, O Lord, our holy fathers and archbishops who from the holy apostle James, Brother of the Lord, to this day were Orthodox archbishops of the holy church of our God in Thy holy city.

Remember, O Lord, our holy fathers and teachers Clement, Timothy, Ignatius, Dionysius, Irenaeus, Peter, Gregory, Alexander, Eustathius, Athanasius, Basil, Gregory, Gregory, Ambrose, Amphilochius, Liberius, Damasus, John, Epiphanius, Theophilus, Celestine, Augustine, Cyril, Leo, Proclus, Proterius, Felix, Hormisdas, Eulogius, Martin, Agatho, and Sophronius.

Remember, O Lord, the seven holy, and great, and ecumenical Councils and the other holy councils and bishops who in all the world in an Orthodox manner have rightly divided the word of the truth.

Remember, O Lord, our holy fathers

Ѿе́цъ на́шихъ по́стникѡвъ па́ѵла, а҆нтѡ́нїа, харитѡ́на, па́ѵла, пахо́мїа, а҆м́ѵна, ѳео́дѡра, і҆ларїѡ́на, а҆рсе́нїа, мака́рїа, мака́рїа, сїсѡ́а, і҆ѡа́нна, па́мвы, пи́мена, ни́ла, і҆сі́дѡра, е҆фре́ма, сѵмеѡ́на, сѵмеѡ́на, ѳеодо́сїа, са́ввы, е҆ѵд́ѵмїа, ѳеокті́ста, гераси́ма, пантоле́о́нта, маѯі́ма, ѻ҆н́ѵфрїа, пафн́ѵтїа, а҆наста́сїа, космы̀, і҆ѡа́нна.

Помѧнѝ, гд҃и, ст҃ы́хъ Ѿе́цъ и҆збїе́нныхъ ѿ ва́рваръ въ горѣ̀ синай́стѣй и҆ въ раи́,дѣ и҆ про́чихъ преподо́бныхъ Ѿе́цъ на́шихъ и҆ по́стникѡвъ правосла́вныхъ и҆ всѣ́хъ ст҃ы́хъ, не ꙗ҆́кѡ ѹ҆́бо мы̀ досто́йни е҆смы̀ помина́ти и҆́хъ бл҃же́нство, но ꙗ҆́кѡ тѣ́мъ предстоѧ́щимъ стра́шному и҆ трепе́тному престо́лу твоему̀ моли́тисѧ ѡ҆ на́шемъ ѡ҆каѧ́нствѣ.

Помѧнѝ, гд҃и, пресвѵ́теры и҆ дїа́коны, ѵ҆подїа́коны, и҆ чтецы̀, и҆ е҆поркие́сты, и҆ пѣ́вцы̀, и҆ и҆́ноки, и҆ дѣ́вы, вдови́цы и҆ си́рыѧ, и҆ воздержнники, и҆ и҆́же съ вѣ́рою во ѡ҆бще́нїи ст҃ѣй твое́й собо́рнѣй цр҃кве сконча́вшихсѧ.

and ascetics: Paul, Anthony, Chariton, Paul, Pachomius, Amun, Theodore, Hilarion, Arsenius, Macarius, Macarius, Sisoës, John, Pambo, Poimen, Nilus, Isidore, Ephrem, Symeon, Symeon, Theodosius, Sabbas, Euthymius, Theoctistus, Gerasimus, Pantoleon, Maximus, Onuphrius, Paphnutius, Anastasius, Cosmas, and John.

Remember, O Lord, our holy fathers murdered by the barbarians on the holy Mount Sinai and in Raithu, and the other venerable fathers and Orthodox ascetics, and all thy saints—not because we are worthy to remember their blessedness, but so that they also, standing before Thy dread and fearful throne, may in return remember our wretchedness.

Remember, O Lord, the presbyters, deacons, subdeacons, readers, exorcists, singers, monastics, virgins, widows, orphans, and ascetics: and all who were made perfect with faith in the holy communion of Thy holy, catholic, and apostolic Church.

Помѧнѝ, гд҃и, бл҃гочести́выхъ и҆ вѣ́рныхъ
цр҃е́й кѡнстанті́на и҆ є҆ле́нꙋ, ѳеодо́сїа
вели́каго, маркїа́на, пꙋльхе́рїю, льва̀ и҆
і꙳ꙋстінїа́на, и҆ и҆̀же по си́хъ бл҃гоче́стнѡ и҆
вѣ́рнѡ цр҃твовавшихъ, и҆ всѣ́хъ и҆̀же въ
вѣ́рѣ и҆ печа́ти хрⷵто́вѣ пре́жде ѹ҆со́пшихъ
хрⷵтолюби́выхъ и҆ бл҃гочести́выхъ и҆
правосла́вныхъ мі́рѧнъ.

Здѣ̀ помина́етъ сщ҃е́нникъ ѹ҆со́пшихъ
хрⷵтїа́нъ и҆̀хже хо́щетъ, глаго́лѧ:

Помѧнѝ, гд҃и, и҆ на́шихъ роди́телей, и҆
бра́тїю, и҆ дрꙋ́ги, и҆ сро́дники и҆мⷬкъ.

Си́хъ всѣ́хъ помѧнѝ, гд҃и бж҃е на́шъ, бж҃е
дꙋхѡ́въ и҆ всѧ́кїѧ пло́ти, и҆̀хже помѧнꙋ́хомъ
и҆ и҆̀хже не помѧнꙋ́хомъ правосла́вныхъ.
са́мъ та́мѡ и҆̀хъ поко́й, гд҃и, во странѣ̀
живы́хъ, во цр҃твїи твое́мъ, въ сла́дости
ра́йстѣй, въ ло́нехъ а҆враа́ма, и҆ і҆саа́ка, и҆
і҆а́кѡва, ст҃ыхъ ѻ҆ц҃ъ на́шихъ, ѿню́дꙋже
ѿбѣ́же болѣ́знь и҆ печа́ль, и҆ воздыха́нїе,
и҆дѣ́же присѣща́етъ свѣ́тъ лица̀ твоегѡ̀, и҆
сїѧ́етъ всегда̀.   на́мъ же сконча́ти живо́тъ

Remember, O Lord, the pious and faithful emperors Constantine, Helen, Theodosius the Great, Marcian, Pulcheria, Leo, Justinian, and those who likewise reigned piously and faithfully, and all Christ-loving, pious and Orthodox laymen who departed before us in faith and with the seal of Christ.

Here the priest commemorates the departed Christians, whomever he wishes, saying:

Remember, O Lord, our parents, brethren, friends, and relatives N. and N.

These all do Thou remember, O Lord our God, Thou God of spirits and of all flesh, those Orthodox whom we have remembered and those whom we have not remembered. Do Thou Thyself give them rest there, O Lord, in the land of the living, in Thy kingdom, in the delight of paradise, in the bosom of Abraham, Isaac, and Jacob, our holy fathers, whence sorrow, sadness, and sighing have fled away, where the light of Thy countenance looks over and always shines. And make straight for us the

хрⷭ҇тїа́нскїй и̑ безгрѣ́шный въ мі́рѣ и̑спра́ви, гдⷭ҇и, собира́ѧ ны̀ подъ но́ги и̑збра́нныхъ твои́хъ, є̑гда̀ хо́щеши и̑ ꙗ̑́коже хо́щеши, є̑ди́нъ то́кмѡ без стꙋда̀ и̑ прегрѣше́нїй, є̑диноро́днагѡ ра́ди твоегѡ̀ сн҃а, гдⷭ҇а и̑ сп҃са на́шегѡ і̑и҃са хрⷭ҇та̀, то́й бо є̑́сть є̑ди́нъ безгрѣ́шенъ ꙗ̑ви́выйсѧ на землѝ.

Дїа́конъ возглаша́етъ:

Ѽ мі́рѣ и̑ бл҃госто́ѧнїи всегѡ̀ мі́ра и̑ ст҃ы́хъ бж҃їихъ правосла́вныхъ цр҃кве́й, и̑ ѡ̑ ни́хже кі́йждо принесѐ и̑лѝ въ помышле́нїи и̑́мать, ѡ̑ предстоѧ́щихъ и̑ хрⷭ҇толюби́выхъ лю́дехъ, и̑ ѡ̑ всѣ́хъ и̑ за всѧ̑.
Ли́къ: И̑ ѡ̑ всѣ́хъ и̑ за всѧ̑.

Сщ҃е́нникъ, возглаше́нїе:

Сегѡ̀ ра́ди и̑ на́мъ и̑ и̑́мъ, ꙗ̑́кѡ бл҃гі́й бг҃ъ и̑ чл҃вѣколю́бецъ влⷣка:

Пѣвцы̀ же глаго́лютъ:

end of our lives as Christian, well-pleasing, sinless, and peaceful, O Lord, gathering us at the feet of Thine elect, when Thou willest and how Thou willest, only without shame and transgressions, through Thine only-begotten Son and our Lord and Saviour Jesus Christ, for He is the only sinless one to have appeared on earth.

The deacon says aloud:

A nd for the peace and good estate of the whole world, and of the holy Orthodox Churches of God, and for those for whom each one has offered or whom each one has in mind, for the Christ-loving people here present, and for each and every one.

SINGERS: And for each and every one.

And the priest exclaims:

Through whom, [grant] both to us and to them, as Thou art a good God and Master who lovest mankind.

The singers respond:

Ѡ҆сла́би, ѡ҆ста́ви, прости́, бж҃е, прегрѣше́нїѧ
на́ша во́льнаѧ и҆ нево́льнаѧ, ѩ҆же въ вѣ́денїи
и҆ невѣ́денїи.

Сщ҃е́нникъ же возглаша́етъ:

Благода́тїю и҆ щедро́тами и҆ чл҃вѣколю́бїемъ
хрⷭ҇та̀ твоегѡ̀, съ ни́мже блгⷭ҇ве́нъ є҆сѝ и҆
препросла́вленъ, и҆ со престы́мъ и҆ бл҃ги́мъ и҆
животворѧ́щимъ твои́мъ дх҃омъ, ны́нѣ и҆
при́снѡ и҆ во вѣ́ки вѣкѡ́въ.

Ли́къ: а҆ми́нь.

Сщ҃е́нникъ блгⷭ҇влѧ́етъ лю́ди, глаго́лѧ:

Ми́ръ всѣ̑мъ.

Ли́къ: И҆ дꙋ́хови твоемꙋ̀.

Дїа́конъ и҆зше́дъ и҆ ста́въ на ѡ҆бы́чнѣмъ
мѣ́стѣ, глаго́летъ дїа́конства сїѧ̀:

Па́ки и҆ па́ки и҆ вы́нꙋ ми́ромъ гдⷭ҇ꙋ
помо́лимсѧ.

Ли́къ: Гдⷭ҇и поми́лꙋй.

И҆ ѡ҆ предложе́нныхъ ст҃ы́хъ, небе́сныхъ,
бл҃же́нныхъ,   стра́шныхъ,   честны́хъ,

Loose, remit, forgive, O God, our transgressions, both voluntary and involuntary, done in knowledge or in ignorance.

And the priest says this exclamation:

Through the grace and compassion and love for mankind of Thy Christ, with whom Thou art blessed and glorified, together with Thine All-holy, good, and life-giving Spirit, now and ever and unto the ages of ages.

SINGERS: Amen.

The priest blesses the people, saying:

Peace be unto all.

SINGERS: And to thy spirit.

The deacon goes out and, standing at his usual place, says this litany:

Again and again, and always, in peace let us pray to the Lord.

SINGERS: Lord have mercy.

And for the holy, heavenly, blessed, dread,

бж҃е́ственныхъ даре́хъ, гдꙋ бг҃ꙋ на́шемꙋ помо́лимсѧ.

Ли́къ: Гд҃и поми́лꙋй.

Ꙗ҆́кѡ да гд҃ь бг҃ъ на́шъ, прїе́мъ ѧ҆̀ во ст҃ы́й и҆ пренебе́сный и҆ мы́сленный и҆ дх҃о́вный свой же́ртвенникъ, въ воню̀ бл҃гоꙋха́нїа, возниспо́слетъ на́мъ бж҃е́ственнꙋ́ю бл҃года́ть и҆ да́ръ прест҃а́гѡ дх҃а, помо́лимсѧ.

Ли́къ: Гд҃и поми́лꙋй.

Соедине́нїе ве́ры и҆ прича́стїе и҆ да́ръ прест҃а́гѡ дх҃а и҆спроси́вше, са́ми себѐ и҆ дрꙋ́гъ дрꙋ́га и҆ ве́сь живо́тъ на́шъ хрт҃ꙋ́ бг҃ꙋ на́шемꙋ предади́мъ.

Ли́къ: Тебе́, гд҃и.

Глаго́лемымъ дїа́конствамъ си́мъ,
мо́литсѧ сщ҃е́нникъ:

Бж҃е и҆ о҆́че гд҃а на́шегѡ і҆и҃са хрт҃а̀, великоимени́те гд҃и, бл҃же́нное є҆стество̀, незави́стнаѧ бл҃гость, всѧ́ческихъ бг҃ъ и҆ вл҃ка, сы́й бл҃гослове́нъ во ве́ки веко́въ, се́дѧй на херꙋві́мѣхъ и҆ сла́вимый ѿ серафі́мъ, є҆мꙋ́же предстоѧ́тъ ты́сѧщи

precious, divine Gifts that are set forth, let us pray to the Lord our God.

SINGERS: Lord have mercy.

That the Lord our God, having accepted them upon His holy, noetic and spiritual altar above the heavens as an odor of good fragrance, will send down upon us in return the divine grace and the gift of the All-holy Spirit, let us pray.

SINGERS: Lord have mercy.

Having asked for the unity of the faith and the communion and gift of the All-holy Spirit, let us commit ourselves and one another, and all our life unto Christ our God.

SINGERS: To Thee, O Lord.

While this litany is said, the priest prays:

O God and Father of our Lord Jesus Christ, O Lord of the great Name, blessed nature, bounteous goodness, God and Master of all, who art blessed unto the ages of ages, who sittest upon the cherubim and art glorified by the seraphim, before whom

ты́сѧщѫ и҆ тьмы̀ те́мъ ст҃ы́хъ а҆́гг҃лъ и҆
а҆рха́гг҃лъ вои́нства, принесе́нныѧ ти́ да́ры,
даѧ́нїѧ, плоды̀ въ воню̀ бл҃гоꙋха́нїѧ прїѧ́лъ
є҆сѝ и҆ ѡ҆ст҃и́ти и҆ соверши́ти сподо́билъ є҆сѝ,
бл҃же, бл҃года́тїю хрⷭ҇та̀ твоегѡ̀ и҆ наи́тїемъ
прест҃а́гѡ твоегѡ̀ дх҃а: ѡ҆ст҃и́, вл҃ко, и҆ на́ша
дꙋ́ши и҆ тѣлеса̀ и҆ дꙋ́хи, и҆ косни́сѧ ѹ҆мѡ́въ
и҆ разсꙋдѝ сѡ́вѣсти, и҆ ѿженѝ ѿ на́съ
всѧ́кꙋю мы́сль лꙋка́вꙋ, всѧ́кїй по́мыселъ
сра́мный, всѧ́кое жела́нїе и҆ помышле́нїе
стꙋ́дное, всѧ́кое сло́во неподо́бное, всѧ́кꙋю
за́висть, и҆ го́рдость, и҆ лицемѣ́рїе, всѧ́кꙋ
лжꙋ̀, всѧ́кꙋ ле́сть, всѧ́кое попече́нїе
жите́йское, всѧ́кое любостѧжа́нїе, всѧ́ко
ѕло̀, всѧ́кїй гнѣ́въ, всѧ́кꙋ ꙗ҆́рость, всѧ́кое
ѕлопомнѣ́нїе, всѧ́кое ѡ҆клевета́нїе, всѧ́кое
движе́нїе пло́ти же и҆ дꙋ́ха, ѿчꙋжде́нное
хотѣ́нїѧ ст҃ы́ни твоеѧ̀.

Возглаше́нїе:

И҆ сподо́би на́съ, вл҃ко, чл҃вѣколю́бче
гдⷭ҇и, со дерзнове́нїемъ, неѡсꙋжде́ннѡ,
чи́стымъ се́рдцемъ, дꙋше́ю просвѣще́нною,

stand thousands of thousands and myriads of myriads of holy angels and hosts of archangels; Thou didst accept the gifts, presents, fruits that were brought before Thee for an odor of good fragrance, and hast vouchsafed to sanctify and to perfect them, O Good One, by the grace of Thy Christ and by the visitation of Thine All-holy Spirit: Sanctify also, O Master, our souls, bodies and spirits, and touch our thoughts, examine our conscience, and cast out from us every evil concept, every licentious thought, every shameful desire and consideration, every improper word, all envy, conceit, and hypocrisy, all falsehood and cunning, every distraction of this life, all greed, every vice, all anger and wrath, all remembrance of evil, every blasphemy, and every movement of the flesh and spirit estranged from the will of Thy holiness.

Exclamation:

And vouchsafe us, O Master, Lord who lovest mankind, that with boldness and without con-

непостꙑ́днымъ лице́мъ, ѡ҆сще́нными ᲂу҆стꙑ̀
сме́ти призꙑва́ти тебѐ, и҆́же на небесѣ́хъ
ста́гѡ бга, ѻ҆ц҃а̀, и҆ глаго́лати:

Лю́діе:

Ѻ҆́ч҃е на́шъ: и҆́же є҆сѝ на нб҃сѣ́хъ, да свѧти́тсѧ
и҆́мѧ твоѐ, да прїи́детъ црⷭ҇твїе твоѐ: да
бꙋ́детъ во́лѧ твоѧ̀, ꙗ҆́кѡ на нб҃сѝ и҆ на
землѝ. хлѣ́бъ на́шъ насꙋ́щный да́ждь на́мъ
дне́сь, и҆ ѡ҆ста́ви на́мъ до́лги на́ша, ꙗ҆́коже
и҆ мꙑ̀ ѡ҆ставлѧ́емъ должникѡ́мъ на́шꙑмъ:
и҆ не введѝ на́съ во и҆скꙋше́нїе, но и҆зба́ви
на́съ ѿ лꙋка́вагѡ.

Глаго́лемꙋ семꙋ̀, сще́нникъ
мо́литсѧ си́цѣ та́йнѡ:

И҆ не введѝ на́съ во и҆скꙋше́нїе, гдⷭ҇и, гдⷭ҇и
си́лъ, є҆го́же понестѝ не мо́жемъ,
вѣ́дый не́мощь на́шꙋ, но и҆зба́ви на́съ ѿ
лꙋка́вагѡ, и҆ ѿ дѣ́лъ є҆гѡ̀, и҆ ѿ всѧ́кїѧ
напа́сти и҆ ко́зни тогѡ̀, и҆́мене твоегѡ̀
ра́ди ста́гѡ, и҆́же нарица́етсѧ на на́шемъ
смире́нїи.

demnation, with a pure heart and illumined soul, with face unashamed and sanctified lips, we may dare to call upon Thee, holy God, the Father who art in the heavens, and to say:

People:

Our Father who art in the heavens, hallowed be Thy name, Thy kingdom come, Thy will be done on earth as it is in heaven. Give us this day our daily bread, and forgive us our debts as we forgive our debtors, and lead us not into temptation, but deliver us from the evil one.

While this is being said,
the priest prays thus silently:

And lead us not into temptation, O Lord, Thou Lord of hosts, whom we are unable to withstand, who knowest our weakness, but deliver us from the evil one and from his works, and from all his oppression and his craftiness, for the sake of Thy holy name which is invoked upon our humility.

Возглаше́ніе:

Я҆́кѡ твоѐ є҆́сть црⷭ҇тво, и҆ си́ла, и҆ сла́ва, Ѻ҆ц҃а̀ и҆ сн҃а и҆ ста́гѡ дх҃а, ны́нѣ и҆ при́снѡ и҆ во вѣ́ки вѣкѡ́въ.

Ли́къ: А҆ми́нь.

Сщⷭ҇е́нникъ: Ми́ръ всѣ҇мъ.

Ли́къ: И҆ ду́хови твоему̀.

Дїа́конъ: Главы̑ на́ша гдⷭ҇еви приклони́мъ.

Ли́къ: Тебѣ̀ гдⷭ҇и.

Сщⷭ҇е́нникъ сію̀ мл҃тву
глаго́летъ та́йнѡ:

Т҆ебѣ̀ приклони́хомъ, раби̑ твоѧ̑, своѧ̑ вы́и предъ ст҃ы́мъ твои́мъ же́ртвенникомъ, ча́ющїе ѿ тебѐ бога́тыѧ ми́лости: бога́тую и҆ ны́нѣ блгⷣть твою̀ и҆ блгⷭ҇ове́нїе твоѐ посли́ на́мъ, влⷣко, и҆ ѡ҆ст҃ѝ ду́ши на́ша и҆ тѣлеса̀ и҆ ду́хи, я҆́кѡ да досто́йны бу́демъ ѡ҆бщницы и҆ прича́стницы бы́ти ст҃ы́хъ твои́хъ та́инъ во ѡ҆ставле́нїе грѣхѡ́въ и҆ въ жи́знь вѣ́чную.

Exclamation:

For Thine is the kingdom, and the power, and the glory: of the Father and of the Son and of the Holy Spirit, now and ever and unto the ages of ages.

SINGERS: Amen.

PRIEST: Peace be unto all.

SINGERS: And to thy spirit.

DEACON: Let us bow our heads unto the Lord.

SINGERS: To Thee, O Lord.

The priest says the prayer silently:

To Thee, we Thy servants have bowed our necks before Thy holy altar, awaiting from Thee abundant mercies; send down also upon us now, O Master, Thine abundant grace and Thy blessing, and sanctify our souls, bodies, and spirits, that we may become worthy to be communicants and partakers of Thy Holy Mysteries unto the remission of sins and life everlasting.

Возглаше́нїе:

Ты̀ бо покланꙗ́емый и҆ сла́вимый є҆сѝ, бг҃ъ
на́шъ, и҆ є҆диноро́дный тво́й сн҃ъ, и҆ дх҃ъ
тво́й прест҃ы́й, ны́нѣ и҆ при́снѡ и҆ во вѣ́ки
вѣкѡ́въ.

Ли́къ: а҆ми́нь.

Сщ҃е́нникъ, ѡ҆бра́щьсꙗ ко ст҃ы́мъ две́ремъ
и҆ бл҃гословлꙗ́ѧ лю́ди, глаго́летъ:

И҆ да бꙋ́детъ бл҃года́ть и҆ ми́лости ст҃ы́ѧ,
є҆диносꙋ́щныѧ, несозда́нныѧ, неразлѣ́льныѧ
и҆ покланꙗ́емыѧ трⷪ҇цы со всѣ́ми ва́ми.

Ли́къ: И҆ со дꙋ́хомъ твои́мъ.

Взе́мъ ст҃ы́й а҆́гнецъ,
сщ҃е́нникъ мо́лится та́йнѡ:

Ѻ҆́ч҃е, во ст҃ы́хъ почива́ѧй гдⷭ҇и, ѡ҆ст҃и́ ны̀
словомъ твоеѧ̀ бл҃года́ти и҆ наи́тїемъ
всест҃а́гѡ твоегѡ̀ дх҃а, ты̀ бо ре́клъ є҆сѝ,
влⷣко: ст҃и бꙋ́дите, ꙗ҆́коже а҆́зъ ст҃ъ є҆́смь,
гдⷭ҇ь бг҃ъ на́шъ.

И҆ присовокꙋплѧ́етъ мл҃твꙋ сїю̀:

Exclamation:

For Thou art worshipped and glorified, O our God, Thou and Thine Only-begotten Son, and Thine All-holy Spirit, now and ever and unto the ages of ages.

SINGERS: Amen.

The priest says, turning to the holy doors and blessing the people:

And may the grace and mercies of the holy, consubstantial, uncreated, indivisible, and adorable Trinity be with you all.

SINGERS: And with Thy spirit.

The priest takes the holy Lamb and prays silently:

O Holy Lord who restest in the holy place, make us holy by the word of Thy grace and by the visitation of Thine All-holy Spirit, for Thou hast said, O Master: 'Be holy, for I AM holy,' the Lord our God.

And he adds this prayer:

Неизрече́нне бж҃е сло́ве, ѻ҆ц҃у̀ и҆ прест҃о́му дх҃у є҆диносу́щне и҆ соприсносу́щне и҆ нераздѣ́льне, прїимѝ нетлѣ́нную пѣ́снь во ст҃ы́хъ твои́хъ безкро́вныхъ же́ртвахъ съ херуві́мы и҆ серафі́мы и҆ ѿ менѐ грѣ́шнаго, вопїю́ща и҆ глаго́люща:

Дїа́конъ возглаша́етъ:

Со стра́хомъ бж҃їимъ во́нмемъ.

Возно́ситъ же сщ҃е́нникъ ст҃ы́й а҆́гнецъ, и҆ возглаша́етъ:

Ст҃а́я ст҃ы́мъ.

Ли́къ: Є҆ди́нъ ст҃ъ, є҆ди́нъ гдⷭ҇ь, і҆и҃съ хрⷭ҇то́съ, во сла́ву бг҃а ѻ҆ц҃а̀ со ст҃ы́мъ дх҃омъ, є҆му́же сла́ва во вѣ́ки вѣкѡ́въ, а҆ми́нь.

Й затворя́ютса ст҃ы̑а двє́ри и҆ завѣ́са.

Дїа́конъ же, ста́въ на ѡ҆бы́чнѣмъ мѣ́стѣ, глаго́летъ проше́нїе сїѐ:

O ineffable God and Word, consubstantial with the Father and the Holy Spirit, co-eternal and indivisible: accept this incorrupt hymn at Thy holy bloodless sacrifices with the Cherubim and the Seraphim, and also from me, a sinner, crying out and saying:

Deacon:
With the fear of God, let us attend.

The priest elevates the
holy Lamb and exclaims:

Holy things unto the holy.
SINGERS: One is holy, one is Lord: Jesus Christ, to the glory of God the Father, with the Holy Spirit, to whom be glory unto the ages of ages. Amen.

And the holy doors and
the curtain are closed.

The deacon, standing at the usual place,
says this petition:

Ѡ҆ ѡ҆ставле́нїи грѣхѡ́въ на́шихъ, и҆
ѡ҆ ѡ҆чище́нїи дꙋ́шъ на́шихъ, и҆
ѡ҆ спасе́нїи и҆ застꙋпле́нїи ст҃а́гѡ ѻ҆тца̀
на́шегѡ, а҆рхїе҆пⷭкопа (и҆лѝ митрополі́та)
и҆м҃къ, всегѡ̀ при́чта и҆ хрⷭтолюби́выхъ
люде́й, и҆ ѡ҆ вся́кой дꙋшѝ хрⷭтїа́нстѣй, скор-
бя́щей же и҆ ѡ҆ѕлобле́ннѣй, ми́лости бж҃їѧ
и҆ по́мощи требꙋ́ющей, и҆ ѡ҆ ѡ҆браще́нїи
заблꙋ́ждшихъ, и҆сцѣле́нїи болѧ́щихъ,
свобожде́нїи плѣне́нныхъ, па́мѧти и҆
оу҆поко́е҆нїи преподо́бныхъ ѻ҆те́цъ на́шихъ и҆
бра́тїй, и҆ всѣ́хъ хрⷭтїа́нъ правосла́вныхъ, всѝ
прилѣ́жнѡ рце́мъ: гдⷭи поми́лꙋй.

Ли́къ: Гдⷭи поми́лꙋй, в҃і.

Дїа́конъ: Въ ми́рѣ хрⷭто́вѣ по́имъ.

И҆ вхо́дитъ во ст҃ы́й ѻ҆лта́рь.

Пѣвцы̀ же пою́тъ прича́стенъ: вкꙋси́те
и҆ ви́дите, ꙗ҆́кѡ бл҃гъ гдⷭь. А҆ллилꙋ́їа, со
стиха́ми ѱалма̀ л҃г: Бл҃гословлю̀ гдⷭа на
вся́кое вре́мѧ.

Е҆гда̀ же глаго́летъ дїа́конъ проше́нїѧ сїѧ̑,
сщ҃е́нникъ преломля́етъ ст҃ы́й хлѣ́бъ на

For the remission of our sins and for the propitiation of our souls, and for the salvation and protection of our holy father, Archbishop [or Metropolitan] N., all the clergy and Christ-loving people, and for every Christian soul that is afflicted and tormented, in need of mercy and help of God, for the conversion of those who are deceived, the healing of the sick, the liberation of prisoners, the memory and repose of our venerable fathers and brethren, and of all Orthodox Christians, let us all fervently say: Lord, have mercy.

SINGERS: Lord have mercy (12 times).

DEACON: In the peace of Christ, let us sing!

And he enters the holy sanctuary.

The singers chant the communion verse Taste and see that the Lord is good. Alleluia with the verses of Psalm 33: I will bless the Lord at all times . . .

While the diaconal petitions are being said, the priest breaks the Holy Bread in twain,

дв҃ѣ̀ ча́сти, пе́рвѣе зна́менавъ ✠ є҆̀гѡ̀, и҆
де́ржитъ десни́цею ча́сть и҆ шꙋ́йцею ча́сть.

И҆ раздробла́етъ ст҃ы́й а҆́гнецъ по ѻ҆бы́чаю,
ꙗ҆́коже оу҆каза́са въ послѣ́довані́и слꙋ́жбы
ст҃а́гѡ і҆ѡа́нна златоꙋ́стагѡ.

Пре́жде всѣ́хъ же, взе́мъ є҆ди́нꙋ ча́сть
ст҃а́гѡ хлѣ́ба, ꙗ҆́же і҃ИС, и҆ зна́менавъ
ю҆̀ ✠, влага́етъ ю҆̀ въ ст҃ы́й поти́ръ,
глаго́ла сло́во соедине́ні́а:

Соедине́ні́е прест҃а́гѡ тѣ́ла и҆ чⷭтны́а кро́ве
гдⷭа и҆ бг҃а и҆ сп҃са на́шегѡ і҃иса хрⷭта̀. Соедини́са
и҆ ѡ҆ст҃и́са и҆ соверши́са во и҆́ма ѻ҆ц҃а̀ и҆ сн҃а
и҆ ст҃а́гѡ дх҃а.

И҆ па́ки глаго́летъ:

Сѐ а҆́гнецъ бж҃і́й, взе́млай грѣ́хъ мі́ра,
закла́нный за мі́рскі́й живо́тъ и҆ спасе́ні́е.

И҆ бл҃гослова́етъ сщ҃е́нникъ
теплотꙋ̀ и҆ влива́етъ ю҆̀ внꙋ́трь
ст҃ы́а ча́ши по ѻ҆бы́чаю.

after signing ✠ it first, and holds each
part in his right and left hands.

And he divides the holy Lamb according
to custom, as it is prescribed in the order of
the Liturgy of St John Chrysostom.

And first, taking one portion of the
holy Bread, i.e. IC, and signing it ✠,
he places it into the holy chalice,
saying this prayer of the union:

The union of the most holy Body and the precious Blood of our Lord, God, and Saviour Jesus Christ. It has been united, and sanctified,
and fulfilled in the name of the Father and of
the Son and of the Holy Spirit.

And again he says:

Behold, the Lamb of God, which taketh away
the sin of the world, slain for the life of the
world and its salvation.

And the priest pours the hot water into
the chalice, according to custom.

И҆ а҆́бїе раздробла́етъ ча́стицы ст҃а́гѡ
хлѣ́ба, по ѡ҆бы́чаю, и҆ прїꙋготовла́етъ
ча́стицы коемꙋ́ждо ѿ сослꙋжа́щихъ,
глаго́ла:

Ча́сть ст҃а́а хрⷭ҇то́ва, и҆спо́лнена бл҃года́ти и҆
и҆́стины, ѻ҆ц҃а̀ и҆ сн҃а и҆ ст҃а́гѡ дх҃а, є҆мꙋ́же
сла́ва и҆ держа́ва во вѣ́ки вѣкѡ́въ.

Є҆гда̀ же прїꙋгото́витъ сщ҃е́нникъ
ча́стицы во є҆́же причасти́ти сослꙋжа́щїѧ,
глаго́летъ дїа́конъ: Го́споди, бл҃гослови́.

Сщ҃е́нникъ: Бл҃гослове́нъ бг҃ъ, бл҃гословла́ѧй
и҆ ѡ҆сщ҃а́ѧй на́съ и҆́же во стра́сѣ бж҃їи
раздробла́ющихъ и҆ всѣ́хъ вѣ́рою при_
части́тисѧ хотѧ́щихъ преⷱ҇ты́хъ та̑инъ гдⷭ҇а
и҆ бг҃а и҆ сп҃са на́шегѡ і҆и҃са хрⷭ҇та̀, ны́нѣ и҆
при́снѡ и҆ во вѣ́ки вѣкѡ́въ.

И҆ ѿвѣща́ютъ всѝ клири́ки: а҆ми́нь.

И҆ глаго́летъ мл҃твꙋ сїю̀,
пре́жде ст҃а́гѡ причаще́нїѧ:

And at once he divides the particles
of the holy bread, according to custom.
And he prepares the particles for each
of the concelebrants, saying:

The holy portion of Christ, full of grace
and truth, of the Father and of the Son and
the Holy Spirit, to whom belongs glory and
power unto the ages of ages.

And when the priest prepares the particles
for the communion of the concelebrants,
the deacon says: Lord, bless.

PRIEST: Blessed is God who blesses and sanctifies us who in the fear of God are dividing
the holy things, and all who with faith are
about to partake of the most pure mysteries
of our Lord, God, and Saviour Jesus Christ,
now and ever and unto the ages of ages.

And all clergy respond: Amen.

And the priest says this prayer,
before the holy communion:

Ꙗ҆́кѡ хрⷭте́ бж҃е на́шъ, нбⷭный хлѣ́бе, пи́ще всегѡ̀ мі́ра, согрѣ́шихъ на нб҃о и҆ пред̾ тобо́ю, и҆ нѣ́смь досто́инъ причасти́тисѧ ст҃ы́хъ и҆ пречⷭтыхъ твои́хъ та́инъ, но ра́ди бл҃гости твоеѧ̀ и҆ неи҆зрече́ннагѡ долготерпѣ́нїа, досто́йна мѧ̀ сотворѝ и҆ неѡсꙋжде́нна и҆ непосты̀дна причасти́тисѧ прест҃а́гѡ тѣ́ла и҆ чⷭтны́ѧ кро́ве во ѡ҆ставле́нїе грѣхѡ́въ и҆ въ жи́знь вѣ́чнꙋю, а҆ми́нь.

Та́же творѧ́тъ во ст҃о́мъ ѻ҆лтарѣ̀ ст҃о́е причⷭтїе бж҃е́ственныхъ дарѡ́въ.

Пре́жде глаго́летъ дїа́конъ сослꙋжа́щимъ сщ҃е́нникѡмъ, а҆́ще сꙋ́ть:

Пресвѵ́тери, пристꙋпи́те.

И҆ глаго́летъ кі́ждо ѿ сщ҃е́нникѡ́въ, прїе́млѧ ст҃о́е тѣ́ло: Тѣ́ло хрⷭто́во.

А҆́ще сꙋ́ть мно́зїи дїа́конни, глаго́летъ протодїа́конъ: Дїа́конни, пристꙋ́пимъ.

O Master Christ our God, the heavenly Bread, Food of the whole world, I have sinned before heaven and before Thee, and I am not worthy to partake of Thy holy and most pure mysteries, but for the sake of Thy goodness and Thine ineffable longsuffering, make me worthy, without condemnation or shame, to partake of Thy most holy Body and precious Blood unto the remission of sins and life everlasting. Amen.

Then in the sanctuary they receive the holy communion of the divine Gifts.

First, the deacon says to the concelebrating priest, if there be any:

Presbyters, draw nigh.

And each of the priests says, receiving the holy Body: The Body of Christ.

If there are many deacons, the protodeacon says: Deacons, let us draw nigh.

Сщ҃éнникъ же преподаéтъ коемꙋ́ждо
дїáконꙋ ст҃óе тѣ́ло, глагóла:
Тѣ́ло хрⷭтóво.

Й ѿвѣща́етъ прїéмлай: а҆ми́нь.

Й причаща́етсѧ кíйждо ѿ сщ҃éнникѡвъ
ст҃ы́ѧ крóве, глагóла:
Крóвь хрⷭтóва, ча́ша жи́зни.

Й причаща́етъ дїáкона глагóла:
Крóвь хрⷭтóва, ча́ша жи́зни.

Й ѿвѣща́етъ причаща́ѧйсѧ: а҆ми́нь.

А҆́ще сꙋ́ть мнóзїи дїáкони, причаща́етъ
коегóждо ѿ дїáконѡвъ та́кожде.

По причащéнïи же сослꙋжа́щихъ, є҆гда́
же прїéмлетъ сщ҃éнникъ ст҃ы́й ді́скосъ,
глагóлетъ дїáконъ: Гóсподи, бл҃гословѝ.
Сщ҃éнникъ: Сла́ва бг҃ꙋ, ѡ҆ст҃и́вшꙋ и҆ ѡ҆сщ҃а́ющꙋ
на́съ.

Й па́ки глагóлетъ:

Вознеси́сѧ на небеса̀, бж҃е, и҆ по всéй землѝ

The priest gives the holy Body to each deacon, saying: The Body of Christ.

And he that receives responds: Amen.

And each of the priests partakes of the holy Blood, saying: The Blood of Christ, the cup of life.

And the priest gives communion to the deacon, saying: The Blood of Christ, the cup of life.

And he that partakes, responds: Amen.

If there are many deacons, the priest gives communion to them all in the same manner.

After the communion of the concelebrants, when the priest takes the holy diskos, the deacon says: Lord, bless.

PRIEST: Glory be to God who blesses and sanctifies us.

And he says further:

Be Thou exalted above the heavens, O God, and Thy glory above all the earth, and Thy

сла́ва твоѧ̀, и҆ црⷭ҇тво твоѐ пребыва́етъ во
вѣ́ки вѣкѡ́въ, а҆ми́нь.

И҆ подае́тъ ст҃ы́й поти́рх дїа́конꙋ, глаго́лѧ:
Бл҃гослове́но и҆́мѧ бг҃а на́шегѡ
во вѣ́ки вѣкѡ́въ.

Посе́мъ и҆схо́дитъ дїа́конъ съ ча́шею
во ст҃ы́ѧ двє́ри, показꙋ́ѧ ча́шꙋ
лю́демъ и҆ возглаша́ѧ:

Со стра́хомъ бж҃їнмъ и҆ вѣ́рою пристꙋпи́те.
Ли́къ же пое́тъ: Вкꙋси́те и҆ ви́дите, ꙗ҆́кѡ
бл҃гъ гдⷭ҇ь, а҆ллилꙋ́їа.

Та́же пристꙋ́пают хотѧ́щїе
причаща́тисѧ, и҆ причаща́ютсѧ
по ѡ҆бы́чаю всѝ.

По причаще́нїи же, глаго́летъ дїа́конъ:
Го́споди, бл҃гословѝ.

Сщ҃е́нникъ же полага́етъ ст҃ꙋ́ю ча́шꙋ
на ст҃ꙋ́ю трапе́зꙋ и҆ глаго́летъ:

Сла́ва бг҃ꙋ, ѡ҆ст҃и́вшꙋ всѣ́хъ на́съ. Бꙋ́ди и҆́мѧ
гдⷭ҇не бл҃гослове́но во вѣ́ки.

kingdom shall endure unto the ages of ages.
Amen.

Then he gives the holy chalice to the
deacon, saying: **Blessed be the name of
our God unto the ages of ages.**

Then the deacon goes out with the chalice
through the holy doors, showing the chalice
to the people, and exclaiming:

With the fear of God and faith, draw nigh.
SINGERS: **Taste and see that the Lord is good.
Alleluia.**

Then those who are going to receive
Communion draw near, and partake
according to the custom.

After communion, the deacon says: .
Lord, bless.

And the priest places the chalice upon
the holy table and says:

**Glory be to God who has sanctified us all.
Blessed be the name of the Lord unto the
ages.**

Ли́къ: И҆спо́лни ѹ҆ста̀ моѧ̑ хвале́нїѧ твоегѡ̀, гдⷭ҇и, и҆ ра́дости и҆спо́лни ѹ҆стнѣ̀ мои̑, ꙗ҆́кѡ да воспою̀ сла́вꙋ твою̀. И҆лѝ и҆́ный тропа́рь днѐ.

Сщ҃е́нникъ же бл҃гословлѧ́етъ кади́ло, прїе́млетъ кади́льницꙋ и҆ кади́тъ три́жды, глаго́люще мл҃твꙋ кади́ла сїю̀:

В҃озвесели́лъ ны є҆сѝ, бж҃е, въ соедине́нїи твое́мъ, и҆ тебѣ̀ прино́симъ пѣ́снь благода́рственнꙋю, пло́дъ ѹ҆сте́нъ, и҆сповѣ́дающе бл҃года́ть твою̀, съ кади́ломъ си́мъ: да взы́детъ пре́дъ тобо́ю, бж҃е, и҆ да не возврати́тсѧ вотщѐ, но дарꙋ́й и҆ на́мъ сегѡ̀ ра́ди бл҃гоꙋха́нїе прест҃а́гѡ твоегѡ̀ дх҃а, мѵ́ро пречи́стое и҆ неѿе́млемое, и҆спо́лни ѹ҆ста̀ на́ша хвале́нїѧ, и҆ ѹ҆стнѣ̀ радова́нїѧ, и҆ се́рдце ра́дости и҆ весе́лїѧ.

Возглаше́нїе:

Ѡ҆ хрⷭ҇тѣ̀ і҆и҃сѣ гдⷭ҇ѣ на́шемъ, съ ни́мже бл҃гослове́нъ є҆сѝ, и҆ со прест҃ы́мъ и҆ бл҃ги́мъ

SINGERS: Fill my mouth with Thy praise, O Lord, and fill my lips with joy, that I may sing of Thy glory. Or another Troparion, as appropriate for the day.

Meanwhile, the priest blesses the incense, takes the censer and censes with it three times, saying this prayer of the incense:

Thou hast made us glad, O God, in the union with Thee, and with this incense do we offer unto Thee the song of thanksgiving, fruit of the lips, confessing Thy grace. May it ascend before Thee, O God, and not return empty; but grant to us also, on account of this, the good fragrance of Thine All-holy Spirit, the most pure myrrh that cannot be taken away. Fill our mouths with praise, and our lips with rejoicing, and our heart with joy and gladness.

Exclamation:

In Christ Jesus, our Lord, with whom Thou art blessed, together with Thine All-holy,

и҆ животворѧ́щимъ твои́мъ дх҃омъ, ны́нѣ
и҆ при́снѡ и҆ во вѣ́ки вѣкѡ́въ.

Ли́къ: А҆ми́нь. Бл҃года́римъ тѧ, хрⷭ҇те́
бж҃е на́шъ, ꙗ҆́кѡ сподо́билъ є҆сѝ на́съ
причасти́тисѧ пречи́стагѡ тѣ́ла и҆ честны́ѧ
кро́ве смотре́нїѧ твоегѡ̀ въ жи́знь вѣ́чнꙋю.
А҆ллилꙋі́а (г҃_жды).

Семꙋ̀ же пѣ́ваемꙋ, ѿхо́дѧтъ сщ҃е́нникъ и҆
дїа́конъ ко ст҃о́мꙋ предложе́нїю
и҆ поставлѧ́ютъ та́мѡ ст҃а̑ѧ. Та́же
и҆зше́дъ и҆ ста́въ на ѡ҆бы́чнѣмъ мѣ́стѣ,
дїа́конъ глаго́летъ:

Па́ки и҆ па́ки и҆ вы́нꙋ ми́ромъ гдⷭ҇ꙋ
помо́лимсѧ.

Ли́къ: Гдⷭ҇и, поми́лꙋй.

Ꙗ҆́кѡ да бꙋ́детъ на́мъ причаще́нїе ст҃ы́нь
є҆гѡ̀ во ѿвраще́нїе всѧ́кагѡ лꙋка́вагѡ
дѣѧ́нїѧ, въ напꙋ́тїе живота̀ вѣ́чнагѡ, и҆ въ
причⷭ҇а́тїе и҆ да́ръ ст҃а́гѡ дх҃а, помо́лимсѧ.

Ли́къ: Гдⷭ҇и, поми́лꙋй.

Прест҃ꙋ́ю и҆ пребл҃гослове́ннꙋю, пречи́стꙋю

good, and life-giving Spirit, now and ever and unto the ages of ages.

SINGERS: Amen. We give thanks unto Thee, O Christ our God, that Thou hast vouchsafed us to partake of the most pure Body and precious Blood of Thy dispensation unto life everlasting. Alleluia (Thrice).

> While this is sung, the priest and the deacon proceed to the table of oblation and place the holy Gifts there. Then, the deacon exits the sanctuary and, standing at the usual place, says:

Again and again, and always, in peace let us pray to the Lord.

SINGERS: Lord have mercy.

That the communion of His holy things may be for us a repulsion of every evil thing, a provision for life everlasting and for the communion and gift of the Holy Spirit, let us pray.

SINGERS: Lord have mercy.

Calling to remembrance our most holy,

влⷣчцꙋ на́шꙋ бцⷣꙋ и҆ приснодв҃ꙋ мрі́ю со
всѣ́ми ст҃ы́ми помѧнꙋ́вше, са́ми себѐ и҆
дрꙋ́гъ дрꙋ́га, и҆ ве́сь живо́тъ на́шъ хрⷭтꙋ̀ бг҃ꙋ
предади́мъ.

Ли́къ: Тебѣ̀, гдⷭи.

Сщ҃е́нникъ глаго́летъ мл҃твꙋ сїю̀ та́йнѡ:

Бж҃е мно́гагѡ ра́ди и҆ неи҆зрече́ннагѡ
бл҃гоꙋтро́бїѧ снисше́дый къ не́мощи
рабѡ́въ твои́хъ и҆ сподо́бивый на́съ
причасти́тисѧ сїѧ̀ пренебе́сныѧ трапе́зы,
не ѡ҆сꙋди́ на́съ, грѣ́шныхъ, ѡ҆ причаще́нїи
пречⷭтыхъ та́инъ хрⷭта̀ твоегѡ̀, но сохранѝ
ны̀, бл҃же, во ѡ҆сщ҃е́нїи, ꙗ҆́кѡ да досто́йны
бы́вше престⷢа́гѡ твоегѡ̀ дх҃а, ѡ҆брѧ́щемъ
ча́сть и҆ наслѣ́дїе со всѣ́ми ст҃ы́ми, ѿ
вѣ́ка тебѣ̀ бл҃гоꙋгоди́вшими, во свѣ́тѣ
лица̀ твоегѡ̀, щедро́тами є҆диноро́днагѡ
сн҃а твоегѡ̀, съ ни́мже бл҃гослове́нъ є҆сѝ,
со престꙋ́ымъ и҆ бл҃гимъ и҆ животворѧ́щимъ
твои́мъ дх҃омъ, ны́нѣ и҆ при́снѡ и҆ во вѣ́ки
вѣкѡ́въ.

most blessed, most pure Lady Theotokos and Ever-Virgin Mary with all the saints let us commit ourselves and one another and all our life unto Christ our God.

SINGERS: To Thee, O Lord.

The priest says this prayer silently:

O God who through great and ineffable compassion hast condescended to the weakness of Thy servants and hast vouchsafed us to partake of this table above the heavens, do not condemn us sinners in the communion of the immaculate mysteries of Thy Christ, but preserve us, O Good One, in sanctification, so that having become worthy of Thy Most-holy Spirit, we may find part and inheritance with all the saints who from the ages have been well-pleasing unto Thee, in the light of Thy countenance, through the compassion of Thine Only-begotten Son, with whom Thou art blessed, together with Thine All-holy, good, and life-giving Spirit, now and ever and unto the ages of ages.

Возглаше́нїе:

Ꙗ҆́кѡ бл҃гослови́сѧ и҆ ст҃и́сѧ и҆ просла́висѧ всечестно́е и҆ великоле́пое и҆́мѧ твоѐ, Ѻ҆ц҃а̀, и҆ сн҃а, и҆ ст҃а́гѡ дх҃а, ны́нѣ, и҆ при́снѡ, и҆ во вѣ́ки вѣкѡ́въ.

Ли́къ: А҆ми́нь.

Сщ҃е́нникъ: Ми́ръ всѣ́мъ.

Ли́къ: И҆ дх҃ови твоемꙋ̀.

Дїа́конъ: Главы̀ на́шѧ гдⷭ҇еви приклони́мъ.

Ли́къ: Тебѣ̀ гдⷭ҇и.

Сщ҃е́нникъ сїю̀ мл҃твꙋ глаго́летъ та́йнѡ:

Б҃же вели́кїй и҆ ди́вный, при́зри на рабы̀ твоѧ̀, ꙗ҆́кѡ тебѣ̀ своѧ̀ вы́ѧ приклони́хомъ, простри́ рꙋ́кꙋ твою̀ держа́внꙋю и҆ и҆сполненꙋ бл҃гослове́нїй, и҆ бл҃гословѝ лю́ди твоѧ̀, и҆ сохранѝ достоѧ́нїе твоѐ, ꙗ҆́кѡ при́снѡ и҆ вы́нꙋ сла́вимъ тѧ̀, є҆ди́наго жива́го и҆ и҆́стиннаго бг҃а на́шего, ст҃ꙋ́ю и҆ є҆диносꙋ́щнꙋю трⷪ҇цꙋ, Ѻ҆ц҃а̀ и҆ сн҃а и҆ ст҃а́го дх҃а.

Exclamation:

For blessed, sanctified, and glorified is Thine all-honorable and majestic Name, of the Father and of the Son and of the Holy Spirit, now and ever and unto the ages of ages.

SINGERS: Amen.

PRIEST: Peace be unto all.

SINGERS: And to thy spirit.

DEACON: Let us bow our heads unto the Lord.

SINGERS: To Thee, O Lord.

The priest prays silently:

O great and wondrous God, look down upon Thy servants, for to Thee have we bowed our necks: stretch forth Thy mighty hand, full of blessings, and bless Thy people, and preserve Thine inheritance, so that always and at all times we may glorify Thee, our God who alone art living and true, the holy and consubstantial Trinity: the Father, and the Son, and the Holy Spirit.

Возгла́снѡ:

Тебѣ̀ бо подоба́етъ и҆ до́лжно є҆́сть ѿ всѣ́хъ на́съ вся́кое славосло́вїе, че́сть и҆ поклоне́нїе и҆ бл҃годаре́нїе, ѻ҆ц҃ꙋ, и҆ сн҃ꙋ, и҆ ст҃о́мꙋ дх҃ꙋ, ны́нѣ и҆ при́снѡ и҆ во вѣ́ки вѣкѡ́въ.

Ли́къ: а҆ми́нь.

Дїа́конъ: Съ ми́ромъ и҆ любо́вїю хрⷭ҇та̀ бг҃а на́шегѡ и҆зы́демъ.

Ли́къ: Ѡ҆ и҆́мени гдⷭ҇ни: го́споди, бл҃гословѝ.

Сщ҃е́нникъ глаго́летъ заа҆мвѡ́ннꙋю мл҃твꙋ ѿпꙋсти́тельнꙋю лю́демъ, возгла́снѡ:

Ѿ си́лы въ си́лꙋ ше́ствꙋющіе, и҆ вся́кꙋю во хра́мѣ твое́мъ и҆спо́лнивше бж҃е́ственнꙋю слꙋ́жбꙋ, и҆ ны́нѣ мо́лимся тебѣ̀, гдⷭ҇и бж҃е на́шъ: соверше́ннагѡ чл҃вѣколю́бїа твоегѡ̀ сподо́би на́съ, и҆спра́ви пꙋ́ть на́шъ, оу҆коре́ни во стра́сѣ твое́мъ всѣ́хъ на́съ и҆ помилꙋ́й, и҆ небе́сномꙋ цр҃твїю твоемꙋ̀ досто́йны покажѝ на́съ, ѡ҆ хрⷭ҇тѣ і҆и҃сѣ гдⷭ҇ѣ на́шемъ, съ ни́мже бл҃гослове́нъ и҆

Exclamation:

For to Thee belongs and to Thee is due from us all, every doxology, honor, worship, and thanksgiving, to the Father, and to the Son, and to the Holy Spirit, now and ever, and unto the ages of ages.

SINGERS: Amen.

DEACON: In the peace and love of Christ our God let us depart.

SINGERS: In the name of the Lord. Lord, bless.

The priest says aloud this prayer of the dismissal of the people:

Going from strength to strength and having completed the divine liturgy in Thy temple, now also we pray Thee, O Lord our God: make us worthy of Thy perfect love for mankind, make straight our path, establish us all in the fear of Thee and have mercy on us, and show us worthy of Thy heavenly kingdom, in Christ Jesus our Lord, with whom Thou

препросла́вленъ є҆сѝ, со всест҃ы́мъ и҆ бл҃ги́мъ
и҆ животворѧ́щимъ твои́мъ дх҃омъ, ны́нѣ
и҆ при́снѡ и҆ во вѣ́ки вѣкѡ́въ.

И҆лѝ и҆на́ѧ мл҃тва ѿпꙋсти́тельнаѧ днѐ.

Ли́къ: а҆ми́нь.

Дїа́конъ: Ми́ромъ хрⷭ҇то́вымъ да
сохрани́мсѧ.

Сщ҃е́нникъ же глаго́летъ мл҃твꙋ
коне́чнꙋю возгла́снѡ:

Бл҃гослове́нъ Бг҃ъ бл҃гословлѧ́ѧй и҆
ѡ҆сщ҃а́ѧй, и҆ сохранѧ́ѧй, и҆ покрыва́ѧй,
и҆ соблюда́ѧй, и҆ оу҆мира́ѧй живо́тъ всѣ́мъ
на́мъ причаще́нїемъ ст҃ы́хъ є҆гѡ̀ пречи́стыхъ
и҆ животворѧ́щихъ та́инъ, и҆́хже прїѧ́ти
сподо́бихомсѧ, всегда̀, ны́нѣ и҆ при́снѡ и҆
во вѣ́ки вѣкѡ́въ.

Ли́къ: а҆ми́нь.

По сконча́нїи же бж҃е́ственныѧ литꙋргі́и,
є҆гда̀ вни́дꙋтъ сщ҃е́нникъ со дїа́кономъ
въ дїа́конникъ потреби́ти ст҃а́ѧ,
дїа́конъ гл҃етъ: Гдꙋ помо́лимсѧ.

art blessed and most glorified, together with Thine all holy, good, and life-giving Spirit, now and ever and unto the ages of ages.

> Or another prayer of dismissal
> appropriate for the day.

SINGERS: Amen.

DEACON: May we be preserved in the peace of Christ.

> The priest says the final prayer aloud:

Blessed be God, who blesses, sanctifies, protects, gives peace, and preserves the life of us all through the communion of His holy, immaculate, and life-giving mysteries, which we were counted worthy to receive, always, now and ever and unto the ages of ages.

SINGERS: Amen.

> After the end of the liturgy, when the priest and the deacon enter the diakonikon to consume the gifts, the deacon says:
> Let us pray to the Lord.

Сщенникъ глаголетъ млтвꙋ сїю:

Ꙗ҆ко, дарова́вый на́мъ ѡ҆сще́нїе прїа́тїемъ всестагw тѣ́ла и҆ честны́а кро́ве единоро́днагw сна твоегw, гда, бга и҆ спа́са на́шегw і҆иса хрта: пода́ждь на́мъ и҆ блгода́ть бла́гw твоегw дха и҆ сохрани ны непоро́чны въ вѣ́рѣ, и҆ и҆спра́ви на́съ къ соверше́нномꙋ сыноположе́нїю и҆ и҆скꙋпле́нїю, и҆ вѣ́чномꙋ бꙋдꙋщемꙋ наслажде́нїю. Ꙗ҆кw ты̀ еси ѡ҆сще́нїе и҆ просвѣще́нїе на́ше, бже, и҆ едиоро́дный тво́й снъ и҆ дхъ тво́й престы́й, нынѣ и҆ присю и҆ во вѣ́ки вѣкwвъ. Дїа́конъ: а҆ми́нь. Гдꙋ помо́лимсѧ.

Сщенникъ глаголетъ млтвꙋ сїю:

Млтва внегда̀ потреби́ти стыа да́ры.

Блгодари́мъ тѧ̀, гдн, вѣ́чнагw свѣ́та да́ршвъ пода́телю, промышла́ющагw ѡ дꙋша́хъ на́шихъ и҆ пꙋтеводѧ́щагw стыа твоѧ: да́ждь на́мъ оу҆мныѧ о́чи во еже зрѣ́ти тѧ̀, и҆ оу҆ши во еже слы́шати тѧ̀ единагw, ꙗ҆кw да и҆спо́лнѧтсѧ дꙋ́ши на́ша твое́ю

The Priest reads this prayer:

O Master who hast given us sanctification by the partaking of the All-holy Body and precious Blood of Thine only-begotten Son, our Lord, God, and Saviour Jesus Christ: Grant us also the grace of Thy good Spirit, preserve us blameless in the faith, and guide us to our complete adoption as sons, and to redemption, and to the eternal delights yet to come. For Thou art our sanctification and illumination, O God, Thou and Thine only-begotten Son, and Thine All-holy Spirit, now and ever and unto the ages of ages.

DEACON: Amen. Let us pray to the Lord.

The priest says this prayer:

Prayer for the consuming of the holy gifts.

We give thanks unto Thee, O Lord, bestower of the gifts of light everlasting, who providest for our souls and guidest Thy saints: Give us noetic eyes that we may see Thee, and ears that we may hear Thee alone,

бл҃года́тїю. Вселѝ въ ны̀, бж҃е, се́рдце чи́сто,
да ѹ҆тверди́мсѧ въ бога́тствѣ твое́мъ,
ди́внагѡ и҆ чл҃вѣколю́бца бг҃а. ѹ҆краси́ дꙋ́ши
на́шѧ и҆ ѹ҆́мъ на́шъ, ми́ръ пода́ждь на́мъ,
рабѡ́мъ твои́мъ, бл҃годарѧ́щимъ тѧ̀. Ꙗ҆́кѡ
бл҃гослови́сѧ цр҃тво твоѐ и҆ сла́ва твоѧ̀, Ѻ҆ц҃а
и҆ сн҃а и҆ ст҃а́гѡ дх҃а, нн҃ѣ и҆ при́снѡ и҆ во
вѣ́ки вѣкѡ́въ.

Дїа́конъ: а҆ми́нь.

И҆ потреблѧ́етъ ст҃ы́ѧ да́ры по ѡ҆бы́чаю.

Конецъ ст҃ы́ѧ и҆ бж҃е́ственныѧ
лїтꙋргі́и ст҃а́гѡ сла́внагѡ и҆
всехва́льнагѡ а҆пⷧла і҆а́кѡва бра́та гдⷵнѧ и҆
пе́рвагѡ є҆пі́скопа ст҃ѣ́йшѧ бж҃їѧ
и҆ вели́кїѧ і҆ерⷧли́мскїѧ цр҃кве.

that our souls may be filled with Thy grace. Implant in us a pure heart, O God, that we may be confirmed in Thine abundance, the wondrous God who lovest mankind. Adorn our souls and our mind, give peace to us Thy servants, who give thanks unto Thee. For blessed is Thy kingdom and Thy glory, of the Father, and of the Son, and of the Holy Spirit, now and ever, and unto the ages of ages.

DEACON: Amen.

And he consumes the Holy Gifts in accordance with custom.

End of the Holy and Divine Liturgy of the Holy, Glorious and All-praised Apostle James, Brother of the Lord and the First Bishop of the Most Holy, Divine and Great Church of Jerusalem

Бжⷭ҇твеннаѧ лїтꙋргі́а прежде҆ѡсщ҃е́нныхъ дарѡ́въ ст҃а́гѡ а҆пⷭ҇ла і҆а́кѡва, бра́та гдⷭ҇нѧ пе́рвагѡ є҆пі́скопа і҆ерлⷭ҇и́мскагѡ.

По девѧ́томъ часѣ̀ и҆ и҆зобрази́тельныхъ, начина́емъ вече́рню си́це:

Дїа́конъ: Бл҃гослови̑, влады́ко.

Сщ҃е́нникъ: Бл҃гослове́но цр҇тво ѻ҆ц҃а̀ и҆ сн҃а и҆ ст҃а́гѡ дх҃а, ны́нѣ и҆ при́снѡ и҆ во вѣ́ки вѣкѡ́въ.

Ли́къ: А҆ми́нь.

И҆ затворѧ́ютсѧ ст҃ы̑ѧ две́ри.

И҆ начина́етъ чте́цъ: Прїиди́те поклони́мсѧ, и҆ предначина́тельный ѱало́мъ. По ѱалмѣ́ же є҆кте́нїю не глаго́лемъ, но чте́цъ посредѣ̀ цр҃кве начина́етъ каѳі́смꙋ н҃і. Дїа́конъ же

The Divine Liturgy of the Presanctified Gifts of St James the Brother of the Lord and the First Bishop of Jerusalem

After the Ninth Hour and Typica, we begin Vespers in this manner:

DEACON: Bless, master!

PRIEST: Blessed is the Kingdom of the Father and of the Son and of the Holy Spirit, now and ever and unto the ages of ages.

SINGERS: Amen.

And the holy doors are closed.

The reader begins: O come let us worship, and reads the Opening Psalm (103). After the psalm, we do not say the litany, but a reader in the middle of the church begins the 18th Kathisma. The deacon does not say the

є҆ктеній ма́лыхъ не глаго́летъ, нижѐ
сщ҃енникъ мл҃твы. И҆спо́лньшейсѧ
же кади́смѣ, ли́цы начина́ютъ
Гд҃и воззва́хъ, и҆ пое́мъ стїхи́ры
трїѡ́ди и҆ мине́й, на д҃.

Зрѝ: Стїхи́ры трїѡ́ди пое́мъ бе́зъ
самогла́сна и҆ мꙋ́ченична, и҆́хже
пое́мъ на стїхо́внѣ.

Дїа́конъ же кади́тъ по ѡ҆бы́чаю, хра́мъ
ве́сь. Пѣ́вамꙋ же бг҃оро́дичнꙋ, сщ҃е́нникъ и҆
дїа́конъ со свѣщено́сцы творѧ́тъ вхо́дъ съ
кади́ломъ, по ѡ҆бы́чаю. И҆ ре́кшꙋ дїа́конꙋ
Го́споди, бл҃гослови, глаго́летъ сщ҃е́нникъ
мл҃твꙋ ѡ҆бы́чнꙋю вхо́да та́йнѡ:

В ́ечеръ, и҆ за́ꙋтра, и҆ полꙋ́дне, хва́лимъ,
бл҃гослови́мъ, бл҃года́римъ и҆ мо́лимсѧ
тебѣ̀, влⷣко все́хъ: и҆спра́ви мл҃твꙋ
на́шꙋ, ꙗ҆́кѡ кади́ло пред тобо́ю, и҆ не
ѹ҆клонѝ серде́цъ на́шихъ въ словеса̀ и҆лѝ въ
помышле́нїѧ лꙋка́вствїѧ: но и҆зба́ви на́съ
ѿ все́хъ ловѧ́щихъ дꙋ́шы на́ша, ꙗ҆́кѡ

small litanies, nor does the priest
say the prayers. After the Kathisma has
been finished, the singers begin Lord I
have cried, and we sing stichera from the
Triodion and Menaion, on 6.

Note: We sing stichera from the Triodion,
omitting the Idiomelon and Martyrikon,
which will be sung at the Aposticha.

The deacon censes the temple, as usual.
While the Theotokion is sung, the priest and
the deacon, preceded by the candle-bearers,
make the entrance with the censer, as usual.
And after the deacon says: Lord, bless, the
priest says the prayer of the entrance quietly:

Evening, morning, and noonday we praise
Thee, we bless Thee, we give thanks unto
Thee, and we pray Thee, O Master of all:
Direct our prayer as incense before Thee, and
incline not our hearts unto words or thoughts
of evil, but deliver us from all that hunt after
our souls; For unto Thee, Lord, O Lord, do we

къ тебѣ̀, гд҃и, гд҃и, о́чи на́ши, и҆ на тѧ̀ ѹ҆пова́хомъ, да не посрами́ши на́съ, бж҃е на́шъ. Я҆́кѡ подоба́етъ тебѣ̀ всѧ́каѧ сла́ва, че́сть и҆ поклоне́нїе, оц҃ꙋ̀ и҆ сн҃ꙋ и҆ ст҃о́мꙋ дх҃ꙋ, ны́нѣ и҆ при́снѡ и҆ во вѣ́ки вѣкѡ́въ. а҆ми́нь.

Дїа́конъ: Премꙋ́дрость, про́сти.

Ли́къ: Свѣ́те ти́хїи ст҃ы́ѧ сла́вы:

Посе́мъ пое́мъ тропа́рь входны́й. Дїа́конъ же кади́тъ всѧ̀ по ѡ҆бы́чаю и҆ вхо́дѧтъ въ ѻ҆лта́рь.

Зрѝ: Въ сре́дꙋ и҆ пѧто́къ ст҃ы́хъ постѡ́въ, тропа́рь входны́й, гла́съ д҃:

Ли́къ: А҆ллилꙋ́їа, а҆ллилꙋ́їа, а҆ллилꙋ́їа.

Чте́цъ, сті́хъ: Тебѣ̀ подоба́етъ пѣ́снь, бж҃е, въ сїѡ́нѣ. А҆ллилꙋ́їа:

Сті́хъ в҃: И҆ тебѣ̀ возда́стсѧ мл҃тва во і҆ерли́мѣ. А҆ллилꙋ́їа:

lift up our eyes, and in Thee have we hoped, let us not be put to shame, O our God. For unto Thee is due all glory, honor, and worship: to the Father, and to the Son, and to the Holy Spirit, now and ever, and unto the ages of ages. Amen.

DEACON: Wisdom! Aright!

SINGERS: O Gentle Light of the holy glory . . .

Then the singers chant the Troparion of the Entrance. The deacon censes all as usual, and they enter the sanctuary.

Note: On Wednesdays and Fridays of the Great Forty-Day Fast, this Troparion of the Entrance is sung, tone 4:

SINGERS: Alleluia, alleluia, alleluia.

READER, VERSE: Unto Thee, O God, belongeth praise in Sion. Alleluia . . .

VERSE 2: And unto Thee shall the vow be performed in Jerusalem. Alleluia . . .

Посе́мъ и҆зше́дъ дїа́конъ глаго́летъ
е҆ктенїю̀ сїю̀:

Па́ки преклѡ́ньше колѣ́на, прилѣ́жнѡ
мі́ромъ гдꙋ̀ помо́лимсѧ. Покло́нъ.

Ли́къ: Гдⷭ҇и поми́лꙋй.

Си́лою и҆ ми́лостїю бж҃їею возста́немъ.

Ли́къ: Гдⷭ҇и поми́лꙋй.

Ѡ҆ ми́рѣ всегѡ̀ мі́ра и҆ соедине́нїи
ст҃ыхъ бж҃їихъ правосла́вныхъ цр҃кве́й, гдꙋ̀
помо́лимсѧ.

Ли́къ: Гдⷭ҇и поми́лꙋй.

Ѡ҆ спасе́нїи и҆ застꙋпле́нїи ст҃а́гѡ ѻ҆тца̀
на́шегѡ, а҆рхїепⷭ҇копа (и҆лѝ митрополі́та)
и҆м҃къ, ѡ҆ все́мъ при́чтѣ и҆ хрⷭ҇толюби́выхъ
лю́дехъ, гдꙋ̀ помо́лимсѧ.

Ли́къ: Гдⷭ҇и поми́лꙋй.

Ѡ҆ бг҃охрани́мѣй странѣ̀ се́й, власте́хъ и҆
во́инствѣ є҆ѧ̀, гдꙋ̀ помо́лимсѧ.

Ли́къ: Гдⷭ҇и поми́лꙋй.

Ѡ҆ ѡ҆ставле́нїи грѣхѡ́въ и҆ проще́нїи
согрѣше́нїй на́шихъ, и҆ ѡ҆ є҆́же и҆зба́витисѧ
и҆ сп҃сти́сѧ на́мъ ѿ всѧ́кїѧ ско́рби, гнѣ́ва

After this, the deacon goes out,
and says this litany:

Again and again, on bended knees, let us pray to the Lord. Prostration.

SINGERS: Lord have mercy.

By the power and mercy of God, let us rise.

SINGERS: Lord have mercy.

For the peace of the whole world and the union of all the holy Orthodox churches of God, let us pray to the Lord.

SINGERS: Lord have mercy.

For the salvation and protection of our holy father, Archbishop [or: Metropolitan] N., for all the clergy and Christ-loving people, let us pray to the Lord.

SINGERS: Lord have mercy.

For this God-preserved land, its authorities and armed forces, let us pray to the Lord.

SINGERS: Lord have mercy.

For the remission of our sins and forgiveness of our transgressions, and for our

и҆ нꙋ́жды, и҆ наше́ствїѧ ꙗ҆зы́кѡвъ, гдꙋ̀
помо́лимсѧ.

Ли́къ: Гдⷭ҇и поми́лꙋй.

Ѡ҆ ст҃ѣ́мъ гра́дѣ хрⷭ҇та̀ бг҃а на́шегѡ, ѡ҆
гра́дѣ се́мъ (а҆́ще во ѡ҆би́тели: ѡ҆ ст҃ѣ́й
ѡ҆би́тели се́й) и҆ вся́комъ гра́дѣ и҆ странѣ̀
и҆ вѣ́рою живꙋ́щихъ въ ни́хъ, ѡ҆ ми́рѣ и҆
сохране́нїи и҆́хъ, гдꙋ̀ помо́лимсѧ.

Ли́къ: Гдⷭ҇и поми́лꙋй.

Прест҃ꙋ́ю, пречⷭ҇тꙋ́ю, пребл҃гослове́ннꙋю
влⷣчцꙋ на́шꙋ бцⷣꙋ и҆ приснодв҃ꙋ мр҃і́ю, честны́ѧ
безпло́тныѧ а҆рха́гг҃елы, ст҃а́гѡ і҆ѡа́нна,
сла́внагѡ прⷪ҇ро́ка, прⷣте́чꙋ и҆ крⷭ҇ти́телѧ,
бж҃е́ственныѧ и҆ сщ҃е́нныѧ а҆пⷭ҇толы, прⷪ҇ро́ки
и҆ страстоте́рпцы мч҃ники и҆ всѧ̑ ст҃ы̑ѧ и҆
пра́ведныѧ помѧне́мъ, ꙗ҆́кѡ да мл҃твами
и҆ предста́тельствы и҆́хъ всѝ поми́лованы
бꙋ́демъ.

Ли́къ: Гдⷭ҇и поми́лꙋй.

deliverance and salvation from all tribulation, wrath, and necessity, and the invasion of the nations, let us pray to the Lord.

SINGERS: Lord have mercy.

For the holy city of Christ our God, for this city (if in a monastery: for this holy monastery), and for every city and country, and for those who in faith dwell therein, for their peace and safety, let us pray to the Lord.

SINGERS: Lord have mercy.

Let us call to remembrance our most holy, most pure, most blessed Lady Theotokos and Ever-Virgin Mary, the honorable bodiless archangels, the holy, glorious Prophet, Forerunner and Baptist John, the divine and sacred apostles, prophets, and passion-bearing martyrs and all the saints and righteous ones, so that by their prayers and protection we all may receive mercy.

SINGERS: Lord have mercy.

Сщенникъ же млтвꙋ вечернюю,
по Гди воззвахъ, тайнѡ:

Бгословенъ ꙯ еси гди, влко вседержителю,
просветивый день свѣтомъ солнечнымъ,
и нощь оуꙗснивый зарѧми ѻгненными, иже
долготꙋ дне преити намъ сподобилъ ꙯ еси, и
приближитисѧ начаткомъ нощи: оуслыши
моленіѧ наша и всѣхъ людей твоихъ, и
всѣмъ намъ прости вольнаѧ и невольнаѧ
согрѣшеніѧ. Пріими вечернѧѧ наша
моленіѧ, и низпосли множество милости
твоеѧ, и щедротъ твоихъ на достоѧніе
твое: ѻсѣни насъ стыми твоими агглы,
воѡрꙋжи насъ ѻрꙋжіемъ правды, ѻгради
насъ истиною твоею, соблюди насъ силою
твоею, избави насъ ѿ всѧкагѡ ѻбстоѧніѧ
и всѧкагѡ навѣта сопротивнагѡ.
Подаждь же намъ и настоѧщій вечеръ,
съ приходѧщею нощію, совершенъ, стъ,
миренъ, безгрѣшенъ, безсоблазненъ,
безмечтаненъ, и всѧ дни живота нашегѡ:

The priest reads the Vesperal prayer,
after Lord I have cried, secretly:

Blessed art Thou, O Lord, Master Almighty, who illuminest the day with the light of the sun and dost brighten the night with rays of fire, who hast vouchsafed us to pass the course of the day and to approach the beginning of the night: hear our entreaty and that of all Thy people, and forgive all of us our sins, voluntary and involuntary. Accept our evening supplications and send down the multitude of thy mercy and compassions upon Thine inheritance. Surround us with Thy holy angels, arm us with the weapon of righteousness, guard us by Thy truth, protect us by Thy power, deliver us from every misfortune and every attack of the enemy. Grant unto us also that this present evening, together with the coming night and all the days of our life, may be perfect, holy, peaceful, and sinless, without stumbling or dreams, through the prayers of the holy Theotokos and all the saints who

мл҃твами ст҃ы́а бц҃ы, и҆ всѣ́хъ ст҃ы́хъ ѿ
вѣ́ка тебѣ́ бл҃гоꙋгоди́вшихъ.

Возглаше́нїе:

Твое́ бо є҆́сть, є҆́же ми́ловати и҆ сп҃са́ти
ны̀, бж҃е на́шъ, и҆ тебѣ̀ сла́вꙋ и҆ бл҃годаре́нїе
возсыла́емъ, ѻ҆ц҃ꙋ̀ и҆ сн҃ꙋ и҆ ст҃о́мꙋ дх҃ꙋ,
ны́нѣ и҆ при́сно и҆ во вѣ́ки вѣкѡ́въ.

Ли́къ: А҆ми́нь.

Дїа́конъ: Во́нмемъ.

Сщ҃е́нникъ: Ми́ръ всѣ́мъ.

Чте́цъ: И҆ дꙋ́хови твоемꙋ̀.

Дїа́конъ: Премꙋ́дрость.

Чте́цъ глаго́летъ прокі́менъ по ѡ҆бы́чаю.
Посе́мъ глаго́летъ надписа́нїе кни́ги,
и҆ чте́тъ ѿ быті̀а.

И҆ глаго́летъ прокі́менъ дрꙋ́гій,
и҆ при́тчей чте́нїе.

Зрѝ: Свѣ́тъ хрⷭ҇то́въ въ се́й слꙋ́жбѣ
не глаго́лемъ.

from the ages have been well-pleasing unto
Thee.

Exclamation:

For Thine it is to show mercy and to save us,
O our God, and unto Thee do we send up
glory and thanksgiving: to the Father, and to
the Son, and to the Holy Spirit, now and ever,
and unto the ages of ages.

SINGERS: Amen.

DEACON: Let us attend.

PRIEST: Peace be unto all.

READER: And to thy spirit.

DEACON: Wisdom.

The reader says the Prokeimenon as usual.
Then he announces the title of the book
and reads from Genesis.

Then he says another Prokeimenon,
and the reading from Proverbs.

Note: The Light of Christ is
not said at this liturgy.

Та́же: Споⷣо́би, гдⷭ҇и, въ ве́черъ се́й:

И посе́мъ ли́къ пое́тъ стїхи́ры стїхώвны, ꙗ́же пи́саны сꙋ́ть въ трїώди на гдⷭ҇и воⷥзва́хъ: си́рѣчь, пое́мъ на стїхо́внѣ трїώди самогла́сенъ днѐ, два́жды, съ ωбы́чными стїхѝ, и мꙋ́ченичень, Сла́ва, и ны́нѣ, бгⷪ҇оро́диченъ тогѡ́же гла́са.

И по е҃же испо́лнитисѧ чте́нїемъ и стїхі́рамъ, глаго́летъ дїа́конъ:

Вне́млемъ: па́ки, прекло́ньше колѣ́на, прилѣ́жнω гдꙋ̀ помо́лимсѧ. Покло́нъ.

Ли́къ: Гдⷭ҇и поми́лꙋй.

Си́лою и ми́лостїю бж҃їею воꙁста́немъ.

Ли́къ: Гдⷭ҇и поми́лꙋй.

Ѡ ми́рѣ всегѡ̀ мі́ра и соедине́нїи всѣ́хъ ст҃ыхъ бж҃їихъ правосла́вныхъ цр҃кве́й, гдꙋ̀ помо́лимсѧ.

Ли́къ: Гдⷭ҇и поми́лꙋй.

Then, the reader: Vouchsafe, O Lord . . .

And, after this, the singers chant the
Aposticha, which are found in the Triodion
on Lord I have cried. That is, at the
Aposticha we sing the Idiomelon of the
Triodion, twice, with the usual verses, and
the Martyrikon. Glory . . . Both now . . .
the Theotokion of the same tone.

And, after the readings and Aposticha
have been finished, the deacon says:

Let us be devoutly attentive: again, on bended
knees, let us fervently pray to the Lord!
Prostration.

SINGERS: Lord, have mercy.

By the power and mercy of God let us
rise!

SINGERS: Lord, have mercy.

For the peace of the whole world and the
union of all the holy Orthodox churches of
God, let us pray to the Lord.

SINGERS: Lord, have mercy.

Ѡ спасе́нїи и застꙋпле́нїи ст҃а́гѡ ѻ҆тца̀ на́шегѡ, а҆рхїепⷭ҇копа (и҆лѝ митрополі́та) и҆м҃къ, ѡ все́мъ при́чтѣ и҆ хрⷭ҇толюби́выхъ лю́дехъ, гдꙋ помо́лимсѧ.

Ли́къ: Гдⷭ҇и поми́лꙋй.

Ѡ ѡставле́нїи грѣхѡ́въ и҆ проще́нїи согрѣше́нїй на́шихъ, и҆ ѡ є҆́же и҆зба́витисѧ и҆ спⷭ҇ти́сѧ на́мъ ѿ всѧ́кїѧ ско́рби, гнѣ́ва, нꙋ́жды и҆ возста́нїѧ ꙗ҆зы́кѡвъ, гдꙋ помо́лимсѧ.

Ли́къ: Гдⷭ҇и поми́лꙋй.

Ст҃ы́ѧ, сла́вныѧ а҆пⷭ҇лы, прⷪ҇ро́ки и҆ страстоте́рпцы мч҃ники и҆ всѧ̀ ст҃ы́ѧ и҆ пра́ведныѧ помѧне́мъ, ꙗ҆́кѡ да мл҃твами и҆ предста́тельствы и҆́хъ всѝ поми́лованы бꙋ́демъ.

Ли́къ: Гдⷭ҇и поми́лꙋй.

Ве́чера всегѡ̀ соверше́нна, ст҃а, ми́рна и҆ безгрѣ́шна оу҆ гдⷭ҇а про́симъ.

Ли́къ: Пода́й, гдⷭ҇и.

А҆́гг҃ла ми́рна, вѣ́рна наста́вника, храни́телѧ дꙋ́шъ и҆ тѣле́съ на́шихъ оу҆ гдⷭ҇а про́симъ.

For the salvation and protection of our holy father, Archbishop [or Metropolitan] N., for all the clergy and the Christ-loving people, let us pray to the Lord.

SINGERS: Lord, have mercy.

For the remission of our sins and forgiveness of our offenses, and for our deliverance and salvation from all tribulation, wrath, and necessity, and uprising of the nations, let us pray to the Lord.

SINGERS: Lord, have mercy.

Let us remember the holy, glorious apostles, prophets and passion-bearing martyrs, and all the saints and righteous ones, so that by their prayers we all may receive mercy.

SINGERS: Lord have mercy.

That the whole evening may be perfect, holy, peaceful and sinless, let us ask of the Lord.

SINGERS: Grant this, O Lord.

An Angel of peace, a faithful guide, a guardian of our souls and bodies, let us ask of the Lord.

Ли́къ: Пода́й, гд҃и.

Проще́нїѧ и҆ ѡ҆ставле́нїѧ грѣхѡ́въ и҆
прегрѣше́нїй на́шихъ ѹ҆ гд҃а про́симъ.

Ли́къ: Пода́й, гд҃и.

До́брыхъ и҆ поле́зныхъ дꙋша́мъ на́шымъ,
и҆ ми́ра мі́рови ѹ҆ гд҃а про́симъ.

Ли́къ: Пода́й, гд҃и.

Про́чее вре́мѧ живота̀ на́шегѡ въ ми́рѣ
и҆ покаѧ́нїи сконча́ти, ѹ҆ гд҃а про́симъ.

Ли́къ: Пода́й, гд҃и.

Хрⷭ҇тїа́нскїѧ кончи́ны живота̀ на́шегѡ,
безболѣ́зненны, непосты́дны, ми́рны, и҆
до́брагѡ ѿвѣ́та на стра́шнѣмъ сꙋди́щи
хрⷭ҇то́вѣ, про́симъ.

Ли́къ: Пода́й, гд҃и.

Прест҃ꙋ́ю, пречтⷭ҇ꙋ́ю, пребл҃гослове́ннꙋю,
сла́внꙋю влⷣчцꙋ на́шꙋ бцⷣꙋ и҆ приснодв҃ꙋ
мр҃і́ю, со всѣ́ми ст҃ы́ми помѧнꙋ́вше, са́ми
себѐ и҆ дрꙋ́гъ дрꙋ́га, и҆ ве́сь живо́тъ на́шъ
хрⷭ҇тꙋ̀ бг҃ꙋ предади́мъ.

Ли́къ: Тебѣ̀, гд҃и.

SINGERS: Grant this, O Lord.

Pardon and remission of our sins and offenses, let us ask of the Lord.

SINGERS: Grant this, O Lord.

Things good and profitable for our souls, and peace for the world, let us ask of the Lord.

SINGERS: Grant this, O Lord.

That we may complete the remaining time of our life in peace and repentance, let us ask of the Lord.

SINGERS: Grant this, O Lord.

A Christian ending to our life, painless, blameless, peaceful, and a good defense before the dread judgment seat of Christ, let us ask.

SINGERS: Grant this, O Lord.

Calling to remembrance our most holy, most pure, most blessed, glorious Lady Theotokos and Ever-Virgin Mary with all the saints, let us commit ourselves and one another, and all our life unto Christ our God.

SINGERS: To Thee, O Lord.

Сщ҃е́нникъ глаго́летъ мл҃твꙋ сїю̀ та́йнѡ:

Ꙗ҆́ко гд҃и бж҃е вседержи́телю, пода́вый на́мъ де́нь въ дѣ́ланїе и̑ но́щь во ѹ̑покое́нїе, тебѣ̀ вече́рнее сїѐ бл҃годаре́нїе принося́ще, припа́даемъ, моля́ще тѧ̀ по́дъ твое́ю бл҃года́тїю сохрани́тисѧ на́мъ, преспѣ́ти ѿ младе́нства, пребыва́ти въ совершенїи, проити̑ нынѣ́шнимъ житїе́мъ къ хотѧ́щей сла́вѣ вѣ́чней.

Возглаше́нїе:

Ꙗ҆́кѡ ст҃о и̑ просла́влено є҆́сть всест҃о́е и҆́мѧ твоѐ, Ѻ҆ц҃а̀ и̑ сн҃а и̑ ст҃а́гѡ дх҃а, нынѣ̀ и̑ при́снѡ и̑ во вѣ́ки вѣкѡ́въ.

Ли́къ: А҆ми́нь.

Сщ҃е́нникъ: Ми́ръ всѣ́мъ.

Ли́къ: И҆ дꙋ́хови твоемꙋ̀.

Дїа́конъ: Главы̀ на́шѧ гд҃еви приклони́мъ.

Ли́къ: Тебѣ̀, гд҃и.

The priest says this prayer secretly:

O Master Lord, God Almighty, who didst grant the day to us for our labors and the night for rest, to Thee we offer this evening thanksgiving and we fall down, entreating Thee that we may be preserved under thy grace, may advance from our infancy, remain in perfection, and pass through this present life toward the eternal glory which is to come.

Exclamation:

For holy and glorified is Thine All-holy name, of the Father, and of the Son, and of the Holy Spirit, now and ever and unto the ages of ages.

SINGERS: Amen.

PRIEST: Peace be unto all.

SINGERS: And to thy spirit.

DEACON: Let us bow our heads unto the Lord.

SINGERS: To Thee, O Lord.

Сщ҃е́нникъ же мл҃тв꙼ главоприклоне́нїѧ:

Ꙗ́ко чл҃вѣколю́бче гд҃и, тво́й ми́ръ дар꙼й на́мъ наста́вника, и̑ соблюди́ дꙋ́шы на́шѧ си́лою твое́ю, ꙗ́кѡ да ми́лостїю твое́ѧ бл҃гости досто́йни бꙋ́демъ во ωсщ҃е́нїи и̑ настоѧ́щꙋю но́щь соверши́ти.

Возглаше́нїе:

Ѽ хрⷭ҇тѣ̀ і҆и҃сѣ гд҃ѣ на́шемъ, съ ни́мже тебѣ̀ и̑ сла́вꙋ возсыла́емъ, безнача́льномꙋ ѻ҆ц҃ꙋ, со ст҃ы́мъ дх҃омъ, ны́нѣ и̑ при́снѡ и̑ во вѣ́ки вѣкѡ́въ.

Ли́къ: А҆ми́нь.

Зрѝ: Мл҃твы за̀ ω̑глаше́нныѧ то́кмѡ въ страстно́й седми́цѣ глаго́лемъ.

Дїа́конъ: Ѡ̑глаше́ннїи, гла́вы̀ ва́шѧ гдⷭ҇еви приклони́те.

Ли́къ: Тебѣ̀, гд҃и.

Сщ҃е́нникъ глаго́летъ мл҃твꙋ̀ сїю̀ та́йнѡ:

The priest says the prayer of inclination:

O Master Lord who lovest mankind, do Thou grant us Thy peace as a guide and preserve our souls by Thy power, so that by the mercy of Thy goodness we may be found worthy to complete also this present night in holiness.

Exclamation:

In Christ Jesus our Lord, with whom do we also send up glory to Thee, the Father without beginning, and to the Holy Spirit, now and ever and unto the ages of ages.

SINGERS: Amen.

Note: The prayers for the Catechumens are said only during Holy Week.

DEACON: Ye catechumens, bow your heads unto the Lord.

SINGERS: To Thee, O Lord.

The priest says this prayer secretly:

Бл҃гослови́ ны́нѣ, гд҃и, рабы̀ твоѧ̀ сїѧ̑ ѡ҆глаше́нныѧ, и҆̀хже призва́лъ є҆сѝ зва́нїемъ ст҃ы́мъ въ чꙋ́дный свѣ́тъ твоегѡ̀ позна́нїѧ, и҆ да́ждь и҆̀мъ позна́ти ѡ҆ и҆̀хже ѡ҆глаше́ни бѣ́ша слове́съ оу҆твержде́нїе: и҆спо́лни и҆̀хъ дх҃а ст҃а́гѡ, во є҆́же бы́ти и҆ и҆̀мъ ѻ҆вца́мъ тебѣ̀ и҆́стиннагѡ па́стырѧ, запечатлѣ́ннымъ печа́тїю ст҃а́гѡ твоегѡ̀ дх҃а, ꙗ҆́кѡ да чле́ны честны́ѧ бꙋ́дꙋтъ тѣ́лесѐ цр҃кви твоеѧ̀ и҆ да сподо́бѧтсѧ и҆ въ бꙋ́дꙋщемъ вѣ́цѣ бл҃же́ннагѡ вои́стинꙋ оу҆пова́нїѧ въ цр҃твїи нбⷭ҇нѣмъ.

Возглаше́нїе:

Да и҆ ті́и съ на́ми сла́вѧтъ пречⷭ҇тно́е и҆ великолѣ́пое и҆́мѧ твоѐ, ѻ҆ц҃а̀ и҆ сн҃а и҆ ст҃а́гѡ дх҃а, ны́нѣ и҆ при́снѡ и҆ во вѣ́ки вѣкѡ́въ. Ли́къ: а҆ми́нь.

Дїа́конъ: Съ ми́ромъ и҆зыди́те, ѡ҆глаше́ннїи. И҆̀же бо ко просвѣще́нїю, къ бл҃гослове́нїю пристꙋпи́те. Приклони́те.

Ли́къ: Тебѣ̀, гд҃и.

Bless now, O Lord, these Thy servants, the catechumens, whom Thou didst call with the holy calling to the wondrous light of Thy knowledge, and grant them to acquire the firm knowledge of the words in which they are instructed. Fill them with the Holy Spirit, that they also may become sheep of Thee, the true Shepherd, sealed with the seal of Thy Holy Spirit, that they also may be honorable members of the body of thy Church and may be vouchsafed in the age to come the true, blessed hope of the heavenly kingdom.

Exclamation:

That they also with us may glorify Thy most honorable and majestic name: of the Father, and of the Son, and of the Holy Spirit, now and ever, and unto the ages of ages.

SINGERS: Amen.

DEACON: Ye catechumens, depart in peace. Ye who are preparing for Illumination, draw nigh for the blessing. Bow your heads.

SINGERS: To Thee, O Lord.

Сщ҃е́нникъ, мл҃тву̀ сїю̀ та́йнѡ:

Гд҃и ст҃ы́й, въ вы́шнихъ живы́й и̑
всеви́дящимъ твои́мъ о́комъ всю̀ тва́рь
призира́й, тебѣ̀ приклони́хомъ вы́ю се́рдца
и̑ тѣле́се, и̑ мо́лимъ тѧ̀: прострѝ ст҃у́ю
твою̀ ру́ку неви́димую ѿ ст҃а́гѡ жили́ща
твоегѡ̀, и̑ бл҃гословѝ всѧ̀ ны̀: и̑ а́ще что̀
согрѣши́хомъ, во́лею и̑лѝ нево́лею, я́кѡ
бл҃гъ и̑ чл҃вѣколю́бецъ бг҃ъ простѝ, да́ру́я
на́мъ и̑ ми́рнаѧ бл҃га̑ твоѧ̑.

Возглаше́нїе:

Я́кѡ бг҃ъ ми́лости и̑ щедро́тъ е̑сѝ, и̑ тебѣ̀
сла́ву возсыла́емъ, о̑ц҃у́ и̑ сн҃у и̑ ст҃о́му
дх҃у, ны́нѣ и̑ при́снѡ и̑ во вѣ́ки вѣкѡ́въ.

Ли́къ: а̑ми́нь.

Дїа́конъ: Воз[с]та́ните. Съ ми́ромъ
и̑зыди́те. И́же ко просвѣще́нїю, ѡ̑глаше́нїѧ
поману́вше, со тща́нїемъ собери́тесѧ.
Приступи́те.

The priest says this prayer secretly:

O holy Lord who dwellest on high and with Thine all-seeing eye lookest down on the whole creation, to Thee have we bowed the neck of our hearts and bodies, and we pray Thee: stretch out Thine invisible hand from Thy holy dwelling-place, and bless us all, and if we have sinned in anything willingly or unwillingly, do Thou forgive, as a good God who lovest mankind, granting us also Thy good things of this world.

Exclamation:

For Thou art a God of mercy and compassions, and unto Thee do we send up glory, to the Father, and to the Son, and to the Holy Spirit, now and ever and unto the ages of ages.

SINGERS: Amen.

DEACON: Arise. Depart in peace. Ye that are preparing for Illumination, keeping in mind your instruction, gather with zeal. Draw nigh.

Сщ҃е́нникъ, та́йнѡ:

Ты̀, млⷭ҇тиве бж҃е, наста́вивый чл҃вѣ́ки
тⷯ позна́нїю твоему̀, призва́вый
и҆хъ въ разꙋмѣ́нїе твоеѧ̀ и҆́стины, при́зри
на рабы̀ твоѧ̀ ѡ҆глаше́нныѧ и҆ наꙋчѝ и҆́хъ
ѡ҆правда́нїемъ твои́мъ, ѡумꙋдрѝ и҆́хъ въ
стра́сѣ твое́мъ, сподо́би и҆́хъ сеѧ̀ ба́ни
пакибытїѧ̀ и҆ соединѝ и҆́хъ ст҃ѣ́й твое́й
собо́рнѣй цр҃кви.

Возглаше́нїе:

Ꙗ҆́кѡ подоба́етъ тебѣ̀ всѧ́каѧ сла́ва, че́сть
и҆ поклоне́нїе, ѻ҆ц҃ꙋ и҆ сн҃ꙋ и҆ ст҃о́мꙋ дх҃ꙋ,
ны́нѣ и҆ при́снѡ и҆ во вѣ́ки вѣкѡ́въ.
Ли́къ: а҆ми́нь.

Посе́мъ же чте́цъ глаго́летъ мл҃твы
коне́чныѧ вече́рни:

Ны́нѣ ѿпꙋща́еши: и҆ Трист҃о́е по Ѻ҆́че
на́шъ:
Сщ҃е́нникъ: Ꙗ҆́кѡ твоѐ є҆́сть цр҃тво:
Чте́цъ же: а҆ми́нь. Гдⷭ҇и, поми́лꙋй м҃.

The priest prays secretly:

Thou, O merciful God, who hast instructed men in Thy knowledge, who hast called them to the understanding of Thy truth, look down upon thy servants, the catechumens, and teach them Thy statutes, make them wise in Thy fear, vouchsafe unto them this laver of regeneration and unite them to Thy holy catholic Church.

Exclamation:

For unto Thee is due all glory, honor, and worship: to the Father, and to the Son, and to the Holy Spirit, now and ever, and unto the ages of ages.

SINGERS: Amen.

After the dismissal of the catechumens, the reader says the final prayers of Vespers:

Now lettest thou Thy servant . . . and the Trisagion to Our Father.

PRIEST: For Thine is the kingdom . . .

READER: Amen. Lord have mercy, 40.

Дїа́конъ: Ми́ромъ хрⷵтꙋ̀ воспо́йте.

Ли́къ же пое́тъ стїхі́рꙋ на оу҆мове́нїе рꙋ́къ.

Та́же дїа́конъ:

Да никто̀ ѿ ѡ҆глаше́нныхъ, да никто̀ ѿ непосвꙗще́нныхъ, да никто̀ ѿ немогꙋ́щихъ моли́тисѧ съ на́ми. Дрꙋ́гъ дрꙋ́га позна́йте, дрꙋ́гъ дрꙋ́га оу҆вѣ́дите. Двє́ри затвори́те, про́сти всѝ.

Ли́къ же пое́тъ стїхі́рꙋ во стⷪ҇а́, гла́съ ѕ҃:

Ны́нѣ си́лы нбⷵныꙗ съ на́ми неви́димѡ слꙋ́жатъ: се́ бо вхо́дитъ црⷭ҇ь сла́вы, се́ же́ртва та́йнаꙗ соверше́на дорꙋ́носитсѧ. Вѣ́рою и҆ любо́вїю пристꙋ́пимъ, да причⷶ́стницы жи́зни вѣ́чныꙗ бꙋ́демъ: а҆ллилꙋ́їа [г҃-жды].

Семꙋ́ же пѣва́емꙋ, сщⷷнникъ простира́етъ а҆нтїми́нсъ. Дїа́конъ же кади́тъ стꙋ́ю трапе́зꙋ и҆ ѻ҆лта́рь. По се́мъ ѿхо́дѧтъ въ предложе́нїе

DEACON: Sing ye in peace to Christ!

The singers chant the Sticheron for
the Washing of Hands.

Then, the deacon:

Let none of the catechumens, let none of the
uninitiated, let none of those unable to pray
with us remain! Recognize each other, know
each other! Shut the doors! All upright!

And the singers chant the following
Sticheron for the Holy Things, in tone 6:

Now the powers of heaven with us invisibly
do serve; for behold, the King of glory en-
tereth in. Behold! the mystical Sacrifice is
brought forth, complete. Let us draw nigh in
faith and love, that we may become partakers
of life eternal. Alleluia (thrice).

While this is sung, the priest spreads out the
antimension. The deacon censes the holy
table and the sanctuary. Then they both
proceed to the table of oblation, and the

и҆ ѹ҆мыва́етъ рꙋ́цѣ сщ҃е́нникъ. Та́же
прено́сатъ ст҃ы́а да́ры по ѡ҆бы́чаю:
и҆дꙋ́ще же ничто́же глаго́лютъ.
И҆ вше́дъ, сщ҃е́нникъ поставла́етъ
ст҃а҃а на пр҇то́лѣ, ниче́соже глаго́люще,
и҆ снима́етъ покро́вцы.
Посе́мъ покрыва́етъ возд꙼ꙋ́хомъ
и҆ кади́тъ ст҃а҃а три́жды.

Зрѝ: Ст҃ы́а две́ри же и҆ завѣ́са
до причаще́нїа сщ҃еннослꙋ́жителей
не затвора́ютса.

Сѷ́мволъ вѣ́ры не глаго́лемъ,
но дїа́конъ ста́въ на ѡ҆бы́чнѣмъ
мѣ́стѣ возглаша́етъ:

Ста́немъ добрѣ́: про́сти всн. Ми́ромъ гд꙼ꙋ̀
помо́лимса.
Ли́къ: Гд꙼и поми́лꙋй.

Сщ҃е́нникъ глаго́летъ мл҃твꙋ сїю̀:

Б҃же и҆ влⷣко всѣ́хъ, досто́йны ны содѣ́лай
ча́са сегѡ̀, недосто́йныхъ, чл҃вѣколю́бче,
да ѡ҆чи́стившеса ѿ вса́кагѡ кова́рства и҆

priest washes his hands. Then they
transfer the holy things as usual, saying
nothing as they go in procession.
Having entered the sanctuary, the priest
deposits the holy gifts upon the holy table,
saying nothing, and removes the covers.
Then he covers them with the aer
and censes the holy things thrice.

Note: The Holy doors and the curtain
are not closed until the communion
of the clergy.

We do not say the Creed, but immediately
the deacon stands at the usual place
and exclaims:

Let us stand well: let us all stand aright. In
peace let us pray to the Lord.
SINGERS: Lord, have mercy.

The priest says this prayer secretly:

O God and Master of all, make us, the
unworthy, worthy of this hour, O Thou
who lovest mankind, so that, being cleansed

вса́кагѡ лицемѣ́рїа, соедини́мса дрꙋ́гъ дрꙋ́гꙋ ми́ра и҆ любвѐ сою́зомъ, оу҆тверждѐни тво́егѡ бг҃овѣ́денїа сщ҃е́нїемъ, ѡ҆ гд҃ѣ и҆ бз҃ѣ и҆ спс҃ѣ на́шемъ і҆и҃сѣ хрⷭ҇тѣ̀.

Возглаше́нїе:

Ꙗ҆́кѡ бг҃ъ ми́лости, любвѐ, щедро́тъ и҆ чл҃вѣколю́бїа є҆сѝ, и҆ тебѣ̀ сла́вꙋ возсыла́емъ: ѻ҆ц҃ꙋ, и҆ сн҃ꙋ, и҆ ст҃о́мꙋ дх҃ꙋ, ны́нѣ и҆ при́снѡ, и҆ во вѣ́ки вѣкѡ́въ.

Ли́къ: а҆ми́нь.

Зрѝ: Цѣлова́нїа ми́ра въ се́й слꙋ́жбѣ не быва́етъ.

Сщ҃е́нникъ: Ми́ръ всѣ̑мъ.

Ли́къ: И҆ дꙋ́хови твоемꙋ̀.

Дїа́конъ: Гла́вы̑ на́ша гдⷭ҇еви приклони́мъ.

Ли́къ: Тебѣ̀, гдⷭ҇и.

Сщ҃е́нникъ же мл҃твꙋ главоприклоне́нїа та́йнѡ:

from every guile and every hypocrisy, we may be united to one another in the union of peace and love, confirmed by the holiness of Thy divine knowledge, in our Lord, God, and Saviour Jesus Christ.

Exclamation:

For Thou art the God of mercy, love, compassion, and love for mankind, and unto Thee do we send up glory: to the Father, and to the Son, and to the Holy Spirit, now and ever, and unto the ages of ages.

SINGERS: Amen.

Note: The kiss of peace is not exchanged at this Liturgy.

PRIEST: Peace be unto all.

SINGERS: And to thy spirit.

DEACON: Let us bow our heads unto the Lord.

SINGERS: To Thee, O Lord.

The priest says this prayer of inclination, secretly:

Є҆ди́не гдⷭ҇и и҆ бж҃е млⷭ҇тиве, приклон_
шимъ вы́и своѧ̀ пред̾ ст҃ы́мъ твои́мъ
же́ртвенникомъ и҆ ѡ҆жида́ющимъ ѿ тебѐ
да́ра дх҃о́внагѡ, низпослѝ блгⷣть твою̀ и҆
блгⷭ҇вѝ всѧ̀ блгⷭ҇ве́нїемъ дх҃о́внымъ,
и҆́же въ вы́шнихъ живы́й и҆ на смире́нныѧ
призира́ѧй.

ВОЗГЛАШЕ́НІЕ:

Ꙗ҆́кѡ хва́льно, и҆ покланѧ́емо, и҆ просла́влено
є҆́сть всест҃о́е и҆́мѧ твоѐ, ѻ҆ц҃а̀, и҆ сн҃а, и҆
ст҃а́гѡ дх҃а, ны́нѣ и҆ при́снѡ, и҆ во вѣ́ки
вѣкѡ́въ.
Ли́къ: А҆ми́нь.

Дїа́конъ: Гдⷭ҇и, блгⷭ҇вѝ.
Сщ҃е́нникъ: Блгⷭ҇ве́нъ бг҃ъ, блгⷭ҇влѧ́ѧй
и҆ ѡ҆сщ҃а́ѧй все́хъ на́съ во предстоѧ́нїю и҆
сщ҃еннодѣ́йствїю пречⷭ҇тыхъ є҆гѡ̀ та́инъ,
ны́нѣ и҆ при́снѡ, и҆ во вѣ́ки вѣкѡ́въ.
Ли́къ: А҆ми́нь.

Зрѝ: Глаго́лемымъ дїа́конствамъ си́мъ,
чте́тъ сщ҃е́нникъ моли́твы, ли́стъ 240.

O only Lord and merciful God, send down Thy grace upon those who have bowed down their necks before Thy holy altar and who await the spiritual gift from Thee, and bless us all with a spiritual blessing, O Thou who dwellest on high and lookest down upon the lowly.

Exclamation:

For praised, and worshipped, and glorified is Thine All-holy name: of the Father, and of the Son, and of the Holy Spirit, now and ever, and unto the ages of ages.

SINGERS: Amen.

DEACON: Lord, bless!

PRIEST: Blessed is God who blesses and sanctifies us all to stand before Thy holy altar and to minister His precious mysteries, now and ever, and unto the ages of ages.

SINGERS: Amen.

Note: While this litany is said, the priest reads the prayers on page 241.

Дїа́конъ: Ми́ромъ гдꙋ помо́лимсѧ.

Ли́къ: Гдⷵи поми́лꙋй.

Застꙋпи́, спси́, поми́лꙋй и сохрани́ на́съ бж҃е, твое́ю бл҃года́тїю.

Ли́къ: Гдⷵи поми́лꙋй.

Ѡ свы́шнемъ ми́рѣ и бж҃їи чл҃вѣ́колю́бїи, ѡ є҆диномы́слїи и спсе́нїи дꙋ́шъ на́шихъ, гдꙋ помо́лимсѧ.

Ли́къ: Гдⷵи поми́лꙋй.

Ѡ ми́рѣ всегѡ̀ мі́ра, и ѡ соедине́нїи ст҃ы́хъ бж҃їихъ правосла́вныхъ цр҃кве́й, гдꙋ помо́лимсѧ.

Ли́къ: Гдⷵи поми́лꙋй.

Ѡ спасе́нїи и застꙋпле́нїи ст҃а́гѡ ѻ҆тца̀ на́шегѡ, а҆рхїепⷵкопа (и҆лѝ митрополі́та) и҆мⷬкъ, ѡ все́мъ при́чтѣ и хрⷵтолюби́выхъ лю́дехъ, гдꙋ помо́лимсѧ.

Ли́къ: Гдⷵи поми́лꙋй.

Ѡ бг҃охрани́мѣй странѣ̀ се́й, власте́хъ и во́инствѣ є҆ѧ̀, гдꙋ помо́лимсѧ.

Ли́къ: Гдⷵи поми́лꙋй.

DEACON: In peace let us pray to the Lord.

SINGERS: Lord have mercy.

Help us, save us, have mercy on us, and keep us, O God, by thy grace.

SINGERS: Lord have mercy.

For the peace from above and the love of God for mankind, for oneness of mind and the salvation of our souls, let us pray to the Lord.

SINGERS: Lord have mercy.

For the peace of the whole world, and for the union of the holy orthodox Churches of God, let us pray to the Lord.

SINGERS: Lord have mercy.

For the salvation and protection of our holy father, Archbishop [or Metropolitan] N., of all the clergy and the Christ-loving people, let us pray to the Lord.

SINGERS: Lord have mercy.

For this God-preserved land, its authorities and armed forces, let us pray to the Lord.

SINGERS: Lord have mercy.

Ѿ ст҃ѣмъ гра́дѣ хрⷮта̀ бг҃а на́шегѡ, ѡ цр҃твꙋющемъ гра́дѣ, ѡ гра́дѣ се́мъ (а́ще во ѻ҆би́тели: ѡ ст҃ѣй ѻ҆би́тели се́й), вса́комъ гра́дѣ и́ странѣ̀ и́ и́же правосла́вною вѣ́рою и́ бл҃гоче́стїемъ хрⷮто́вымъ живꙋ́щихъ въ ни́хъ, ѡ ми́рѣ и́ сохране́нїи и́хъ, гдꙋ помо́лимсѧ.

Ли́къ: Гдⷭ҇и поми́лꙋй.

Ѿхрⷭ҇тїа́нѣхъ, приходѧ́щихъйгра́дꙋщихъ поклони́тисѧ во ст҃ы́хъ хрⷮта̀ бг҃а на́шегѡ мѣ́стѣхъ си́хъ, ѡ пꙋтеше́ствꙋющихъ, стра́нствꙋющихъ, и́ въ плѣне́нїи сꙋ́щихъ бра́тїахъ на́шихъ, ѡ ми́рномъ возвраще́нїи коегѡ́ждо и́хъ съ ра́достїю вскорѣ̀ во своѧ̑ си, гдꙋ помо́лимсѧ.

Ли́къ: Гдⷭ҇и поми́лꙋй.

Ѿ ѻставле́нїи грѣхѡ́въ и́ проще́нїи прегрѣше́нїй на́шихъ, и́ ѡ и҆зба́витисѧ и́ сп҃сти́сѧ на́мъ ѿ вса́кїѧ ско́рби, гнѣ́ва и́ нꙋ́жды и́ воста́нїѧ ꙗ҆зы́кѡвъ, гдꙋ помо́лимсѧ.

Ли́къ: Гдⷭ҇и поми́лꙋй.

For the holy city of Christ our God, for the royal city, for this city (if in a monastery: for this holy monastery), for every city and countryside, and those who in Orthodox faith and Christian piety dwell therein, for their peace and safety, let us pray to the Lord.

SINGERS: Lord have mercy.

For the Christians who have come and approach to venerate these holy places of Christ our God, for travelers, those who sojourn in foreign lands, and our brethren in captivity, for the peaceful and speedy return of each one of them with joy to their homes, let us pray to the Lord.

SINGERS: Lord have mercy.

For the remission of our sins and the forgiveness of our transgressions, and for our deliverance and salvation from all tribulation, wrath, and necessity, and uprising of the nations, let us pray to the Lord.

SINGERS: Lord have mercy.

Ѽ є҆́же ѹ҆слы́шатисѧ и҆ бл҃гопрїѧ́тнѹ
бы́ти моле́нїю на́шемѹ пред̾ бг҃омъ, и҆
низпосла́тисѧ бога́тымъ ми́лостемъ и҆
щедро́тамъ є҆гѡ̀ на всѧ̑ ны̀ и҆ ѡ҆ сподо́битисѧ
на́мъ црⷵтвїѧ нбⷵнагѡ, прилѣ́жнѡ мо́лимъ
тѧ̀.

Ли́къ: Гдⷵи поми́лѹй.

Ѽ и҆́хже ст҃ы̑ѧ посты̀ и҆ моле́нїѧ
соверша́ющихъ, и҆ прише́дшихъ поклони́тисѧ
живоно́сномѹ гро́бѹ гдⷵа на́шегѡ і҆и҃са
хрⷵта̀ и҆ помоли́тисѧ во ст҃ы́хъ хра́мѣхъ
правосла́вныхъ, гдⷵѹ помо́лимсѧ.

Ли́къ: Гдⷵи поми́лѹй.

Прест҃ѹ́ю, пречи́стѹю, пребл҃гослове́ннѹю
влⷣчцѹ на́шѹ бцⷣѹ и҆ приснодв҃ѹ мр҃і́ю, честны̑ѧ
безпло́тныѧ а҆рха́гг҃лы, ст҃а́гѡ і҆ѡа́нна,
сла́внагѡ прⷪ҇ро́ка, пⷢ҇те́чѹ и҆ крⷵти́тела,
бж҃е́ственныѧ, сцⷢ҇е́нныѧ а҆пⷵтолы, прⷪ҇ро́ки
и҆ страстоте́рпцы мⷱ҇ники, со всѣ́ми
ст҃ы́ми и҆ пра́ведными помѧне́мъ, ꙗ҆́кѡ
да мл҃твами и҆ предста́тельствы и҆́хъ всѝ
поми́ловани бѹ́демъ.

That our entreaty may be heard and found acceptable before God, and that His plenteous mercies and compassion may be sent down upon us, and that we may be vouchsafed the heavenly Kingdom, let us pray to the Lord.

SINGERS: Lord have mercy.

For those who perform the holy fast and entreaty, and for those who came to venerate the life-bearing tomb of our Lord Jesus Christ and to pray in the holy churches of the Orthodox, let us pray to the Lord.

SINGERS: Lord have mercy.

Let us call to remembrance our most holy, most pure, most blessed Lady Theotokos and Ever-Virgin Mary, the honorable bodiless archangels, the holy glorious Prophet, Forerunner and Baptist John, the divine and sacred apostles, prophets, and passion-bearing martyrs, with all the saints and righteous ones, so that by their intercessions and protection we all may receive mercy.

Ли́къ: Гдⷭ҇и поми́луй.

И҆ ω҆ предложéнныхъ и҆ преждеωсщéнныхъ, чⷮ҇ныхъ, сла́вныхъ, небéсныхъ, та́йныхъ, стра́шныхъ, бжⷭ҇твенныхъ дарѣ́хъ, и҆ сп҃сéнїи предстоѧ́щагω и҆ приносѧ́щагω а҆̀ ст҃а́гω, преподо́бнагω ѻ҆тца̀ на́шегω і҆ерéа [и҆лѝ є҆пи́скопа, и҆лѝ і҆еромона́ха и҆лѝ а҆рхїмандрі́та] и҆́мкъ, гдⷭ҇а бг҃а на́шегω мо́лимъ.

Лю́дїе: Гдⷭ҇и поми́луй (г҃-жды).

Сéй є҆ктенїѝ глаго́лемей, мо́литсѧ сщéнникъ предъ ст҃о́ю трапéзою, преклони́въ главꙋ̀, та́йнω си́це:

Сла́ва въ вы́шнихъ бг҃у, и҆ на землѝ ми́ръ, въ чл҃вѣ́цехъ бл҃говолéнїе. Три́жды.

Гдⷭ҇и, оу҆стнѣ̀ моѝ ѿвéрзеши, и҆ оу҆ста̀ моѧ̑ возвѣсти́тъ хвалꙋ̀ твою̀. Три́жды.

Да и҆спо́лнѧтсѧ оу҆ста̀ на́ша хвалéнїѧ твоегὼ, гдⷭ҇и, ꙗ҆́кω да воспоéмъ сла́вꙋ твою̀, вéсь дéнь великолѣ́пїе твоѐ. Три́жды.

Ѻ҆ц҃а̀ и҆ сн҃а и҆ ст҃а́гω дх҃а, нынѣ̀ и҆ при́снω, и҆ во вѣ́ки вѣкώвъ, а҆ми́нь.

SINGERS: Lord have mercy.

And for the precious, glorious, heavenly, mystical, fearsome divine Gifts set forth and Presanctified, and the salvation of our holy venerable father, priest (or bishop, or hieromonk or archimandrite) N. who presides and offers them, let us entreat the Lord our God.

SINGERS: Lord have mercy. Thrice.

> While this litany is being said,
> the priest prays thus, secretly, before
> the holy table, bowing his head:

Glory to God in the highest, and on earth peace, goodwill among men. Thrice.
O Lord, open Thou my lips, and my mouth shall show forth Thy praise. Thrice.
Let our mouths be filled with Thy praise, O Lord, that we may sing unto Thy glory, and all day unto Thy majesty. Thrice.
Of the Father, and of the Son, and of the Holy Spirit, now and ever and unto the ages of ages. Amen.

Й глаго́летъ сщѣⷩникъ та́йнѡ
мⷧа́твꙋ сїю̀, ста́гѡ і҆а́кѡва:

По҆сѣти́вый на́съ ми́лостїю и҆ щедро́тами,
вⷧа́ко гдⷭ҇и, и҆ дарова́вый дерзнове́нїе на́мъ,
смире́ннымъ и҆ грѣ́шнымъ и҆ недосто́йнымъ
рабѡ́мъ твои҆мъ предстоѧ́ти ста́мꙋ твоемꙋ̀
же́ртвенникꙋ и҆ приноси́ти тебѣ̀ стра́шнꙋю
сїю̀ и҆ безкро́внꙋю же́ртвꙋ ѡ на́шихъ грѣсѣ́хъ
и҆ ѡ лю́дскихъ невѣ́дѣнїихъ, при́зри на
мѧ̀, непотре́бнагѡ раба̀ твоегѡ̀, и҆ простѝ
моѧ̀ согрѣше́нїа твои҆мъ бⷧгоꙋтро́бїемъ,
и҆ ѡчи́сти ми ꙋстнѣ̀ и҆ се́рдце ѿ всѧ́кїѧ
скве́рны пло́ти и҆ дꙋ́ха, и҆ ѿста́ви ѿ менѐ
всѧ́кїй по́мыслъ сра́мный же и҆ неразꙋ́мный,
и҆ ꙋдовлѝ мѧ̀, си́лою всестⷢа́гѡ твоегѡ̀
дꙋ́ха въ слꙋ́жбꙋ сїю̀, и҆ прїимѝ мѧ ра́ди
твоеѧ̀ бⷧго́сти, приближа́ющагосѧ ста́мꙋ
твоемꙋ̀ же́ртвенникꙋ, и҆ бⷧговолѝ, гдⷭ҇и,
прїѧ́тнымъ бы́ти приноси́мымъ тебѣ̀
дарѡ́мъ си́мъ рꙋка́ми на́шими, снисходѧ́ще
мои҆мъ не́мощемъ, и҆ не ѿве́ржи менѐ ѿ
лица̀ твоегѡ̀, нижѐ возгнꙋша́йсѧ моегѡ̀

And the priest says secretly this
prayer of Saint James:

O Master Lord who hast visited us with
mercy and compassion, and hast
granted to us, thy humble, sinful, and unworthy servants, boldness to stand before Thy holy
altar and to offer Thee this dread and bloodless sacrifice for our sins and for the sins of the
ignorance of the people: look down upon me,
Thine unprofitable servant, and blot out my
transgressions on account of Thy tender mercy,
and cleanse my lips and heart from every defilement of flesh and spirit, and remove from
me every shameful and irrational thought, and
by the power of Thine All-holy Spirit make me
sufficient for this liturgy, and accept me for the
sake of Thy goodness as I approach Thy holy altar, and be well-pleased, O Lord, condescend-
ing to my weakness, that these gifts which are
brought forth by our hands may be acceptable,
and cast me not away from thy face, neither
abhor mine unworthiness, but have mercy on

недостоинства, но помилꙋй мѧ бже, по
велицѣй милости твоей, и по множествꙋ
щедрѡтъ твоихъ презри беззакѡнїѧ моѧ,
ꙗкѡ да неѡсꙋжденнѡ пришедъ предъ
стою славою твоею, сподоблюсѧ покрова
единороднагѡ твоегѡ сна и ѡсїѧнїѧ
престагѡ твоегѡ дха, и не ꙗкѡ рабъ
грѣха ѿверженъ бꙋдꙋ, но ꙗкѡ рабъ твой
ѡбрѣтꙋ благодать и милость и ѡставленїе
грѣхѡвъ, въ семъ и бꙋдꙋщемъ вѣцѣ. ей,
влко вседержителю, всесильне гди, оуслыши
моленїе мое: ты бо еси всѧ дѣйствꙋѧй во
всѣхъ, и ѿ тебѣ вси чаемъ во всѣхъ помощи
же и застꙋпленїѧ, и ѿ единороднагѡ
твоегѡ сна и животворѧщагѡ дха, нынѣ
и приснѡ, и во вѣки вѣкѡвъ, аминь.

И молитвꙋ сїю:

Гди вседержителю, неизреченне,
неизслѣдне, непостижиме, недовѣдоме
и несказанне гди, иже единъ имѣѧй
безсмертїе и державꙋ, живый во свѣтѣ
непостижимѣмъ, прїими молитвꙋ

me, O God, according to Thy great mercy, and according to the multitude of Thy compassion pass over my transgressions, that having entered without condemnation before Thy holy glory, I may be made worthy of the protection of Thine only-begotten Son and the illumination of Thine All-holy Spirit; and may I not be cast out as a slave of sin, but as Thy servant may I find grace and mercy and remission of the sins in this age and in the age to come. Yea, almighty Master, all-powerful Lord, hearken to my prayer, for Thou art He that works all things in all, and we seek assistance and help in all things from Thee, and from Thine only-begotten Son and thy life-giving Spirit, now and ever and unto the ages of ages. Amen.

And he adds this prayer:

O Lord almighty, ineffable, unsearchable, incomprehensible, unknowable and unspeakable Lord, who alone hast immortality and power, who dwellest in the incomprehensible light, accept Thou our prayer and

на́шꙋ и҆ проше́нїе и҆ моле́нїе всѣ́хъ ст҃ы́хъ
твои́хъ, и҆ да́ждь на́мъ прежде[ш]сꙴще́ннꙋю
сїю̀ слꙋ́жбꙋ и҆́мени твоемꙋ̀ соверши́ти въ
ча́съ се́й прише́ствїемъ дх҃а ст҃а́гѡ твоегѡ̀,
не въ сꙋ́дъ, нижѐ во ѡ҆сꙋжде́нїе, нижѐ
во ѡ҆бличе́нїе грѣхѡ́въ на́шихъ, но во
и҆сцѣле́нїе и҆ жи́знь вѣ́чнꙋю, во трезвѣ́нїе
и҆ ѡ҆сꙋще́нїе, въ преподо́бїе и҆ по́мощь ꙗ҆́же
ѿ тебѐ гд҃и.

И҆ по е҆ктенїи, глаго́летъ
сꙶще́нникъ возглаше́нїе сїѐ:

Ѡ҆ хрⷭ҇тѣ̀ і҆и҃сѣ гдⷭ҇ѣ на́шемъ, съ ни́мже тебѣ̀
и҆ сла́вꙋ возсыла́емъ, безнача́льномꙋ ѻ҆ц҃ꙋ,
со ст҃ы́мъ дх҃омъ, ны́нѣ и҆ прⷭ҇нѡ и҆ во
вѣ́ки вѣкѡ́въ.
Ли́къ: А҆ми́нь.

И҆ по возглаше́нїи глаго́летъ
дїа́конъ дїа́конства сїѧ̑:

И҆спо́лнимъ мл҃твꙋ на́шꙋ гдⷭ҇еви, ꙗ҆́кѡ
и҆спо́лнь не́бо и҆ землѧ̀ сла́вы е҆гѡ̀.
Ли́къ: Гдⷭ҇и поми́лꙋй.

petition and entreaty of all Thy Saints, and grant us at this hour to fulfill this presanctified liturgy unto Thy name by the coming of Thy Holy Spirit, not unto judgment, nor unto condemnation, neither unto the revelation of our sins, but for healing and life eternal, for vigilance and sanctification, for holiness and protection that are from Thee, O Lord.

And after the litany, the priest
says this exclamation:

In Christ Jesus, our Lord, with whom to Thee do we send up glory, to the Father who is without beginning, and with the Holy Spirit, now and ever, and unto the ages of ages.
SINGERS: Amen.

After the exclamation, the deacon
says this litany:

Let us complete our prayer unto the Lord, for heaven and earth are full of His glory.
SINGERS: Lord have mercy.

И҆ ѡ҆ предложе́нныхъ и҆ прежде[ш]сщ҃е́нныхъ чⷮтны́хъ дарѣ́хъ, гдꙋ̀ помо́лимсѧ.

Ли́къ: Гдⷭ҇и поми́лꙋй.

Ꙗ҆́кѡ да гдⷭ҇ь бг҃ъ на́шъ, прїе́мъ ѧ̀ во ст҃ы́й и҆ мы́сленный сво́й же́ртвенникъ, въ воню̀ бл҃гоꙋха́нїѧ, возниспо́слетъ на́мъ бж҃е́ственнꙋю бл҃года́ть и҆ да́ръ всест҃а́гѡ дх҃а, помо́лимсѧ.

Ли́къ: Гдⷭ҇и поми́лꙋй.

Соедине́нїе вѣ́ры и҆ прича́стїе ст҃а́гѡ дх҃а и҆спроси́вше, са́ми себѐ и҆ дрꙋ́гъ дрꙋ́га и҆ ве́сь живо́тъ на́шъ хрⷭ҇тꙋ̀ бг҃ꙋ предади́мъ.

Ли́къ: Тебѣ̀, гдⷭ҇и.

Сщ҃е́нникъ, приклонь главꙋ̀,

мо́литсѧ:

Гдⷭ҇и срⷣцевѣ́дче, и҆́же вѣ́си всѣ́хъ человѣ́къ помышле́нїѧ и҆ всѧ́ческаѧ свѣ́дый пре́жде сбытїѧ̀ и҆́хъ, при́зри съ небесѐ посѣще́нїемъ твои́мъ и҆ бл҃гоꙋтро́бїемъ, и҆ поми́лꙋй на́съ, и҆ прїими́ моле́нїе на́ше и҆ проше́нїе, и҆ ѡ҆чи́сти ꙋ҆стнѣ̀ на́ша и҆ дꙋ́шꙋ ѿ всѧ́кїѧ скве́рны дꙋ́ха и҆ пло́ти, и҆ ꙋ҆твѣрди́ ны бл҃гопрїѧ́тны

And for the precious gifts that are set forth and presanctified, let us pray to the Lord.

SINGERS: Lord have mercy.

That the Lord our God, having accepted them upon His holy and noetic altar as an odor of spiritual fragrance, may send down for us in return the divine grace and the gift of the All-holy Spirit, let us pray.

SINGERS: Lord have mercy.

Having asked for the unity of the faith and the communion of the Holy Spirit, let us commit ourselves and one another and all our life unto Christ our God.

SINGERS: To Thee, O Lord.

The priest bows his head and prays:

O Lord who knowest the heart, who dost understand the thoughts of all men, and knowest all things before they come into being, look down from heaven with Thy visitation and deep compassion, and have mercy on us, and accept our entreaty and petition, and purify our lips and soul from all

со дерзнове́нїемъ и ѡчище́нїемъ въ се́мъ
преждеωсψе́нномъ приноше́нїи.

ВОЗГЛАШЕ́НЇЕ:

И да́ждь на́мъ гд҃н, прїе́мный я́кѡ да́ръ
неωсꙋжде́нъ сїѐ преждеωсψе́нное та́инство,
сме́ти и призыва́ти тебѐ, небе́снагѡ бг҃а,
ст҃агѡ ѻ҆ц҃а̀, ми́лостивагѡ, и глаго́лати.
Лю́дїе: Ѻ҆́ч҃е на́шъ:

Глаго́лемꙋ семꙋ̀, сψе́нникъ
мо́литса си́це та́йнѡ:

И не введѝ на́съ во и҆скꙋше́нїе, гд҃н, гд҃н
И҆же ѻ҆те́цъ на́шихъ, но и҆зба́ви на́съ ѿ
лꙋка́вагѡ, и ѿ де́лъ е҆гѡ̀ и҆́мене твоегѡ̀
ра́ди ст҃агѡ, и҆́же нарица́етса на на́шемъ
смире́нїи.

ВОЗГЛАШЕ́НЇЕ:

Я́кѡ твоѐ е҆́сть цр҃тво, и си́ла, и сла́ва,

defilement of spirit and flesh, and confirm us to be acceptable with boldness and holiness in this Presanctified offering.

Exclamation:

And grant, O Lord, who dost accept this Presanctified mystery as a gift, without condemnation, that we may dare to call upon Thee, the heavenly God, the holy and merciful Father, and to say:

PEOPLE: Our Father . . .

While this is said, the priest
prays thus, secretly:

And lead us not into temptation, O Lord, Lord God of our fathers, but deliver us from the evil one, and from his deeds, for the sake of Thy holy name, by which we, the lowly ones, are called.

Exclamation:

For Thine is the kingdom, and the power, and the glory, of the Father, and of the Son, and

Ѿца́ и сн҃а и ст҃агѡ дх҃а, ны́нѣ и при́снѡ и во вѣ́ки вѣкѡ́въ.

Ли́къ: А҆ми́нь.

Сще́нникъ: Ми́ръ всѣ́мъ.

Ли́къ: И҆ дꙋ́хови твоемꙋ̀.

Дїа́конъ: Гла́вы на́ша гд҃еви приклони́мъ.

Ли́къ: Тебѣ̀ гд҃и.

Сще́нникъ сїю̀ мл҃твꙋ
глаго́летъ та́йнѡ:

Тебѣ̀ приклони́ша раби̂ твоѧ̂ вы̂и сердѐ́цъ свои́хъ, ча́юще ѿ тебѐ да́ра дꙋхо́внагѡ и҆ бога́тыѧ ми́лости: бога́тꙋю и҆ ны́нѣ блгⷣа́ть низпосли́ на́мъ влⷣко, и҆ ѡ҆чⷭ́ти дꙋ́ши на́ша, и҆ дꙋ́хи, и҆ тѣлеса̀, ꙗ҆́кѡ да досто́йни бꙋ́демъ ѡ҆́бщницы и҆ прича́стницы бы́ти нбⷭ́ныхъ твои́хъ та́йнъ во ѡ҆ставле́нїе грѣхѡ́въ и҆ въ напꙋ́тїе живота̀ вѣ́чнагѡ.

Возглаше́нїе:

Ꙗ҆́кѡ блгⷭ҇ви́сѧ, ѡ҆ст҃и́сѧ, и҆ просла́висѧ

of the Holy Spirit, now and ever and unto the ages of ages.

SINGERS: Amen.

PRIEST: Peace be unto all.

SINGERS: And to thy spirit.

DEACON: Let us bow our heads unto the Lord.

SINGERS: To Thee, O Lord.

The priest says this prayer secretly:

To Thee Thy servants have bowed the necks of their heart, awaiting from Thee a spiritual gift and rich mercy. Send down upon us now Thy rich grace, O Master, and purify our souls, spirits, and bodies, so that we be made worthy to be communicants and partakers of Thy heavenly mysteries for the remission of sins and for the provision of life eternal.

Exclamation:

For blessed, sanctified, and glorified is Thy name, of the Father, and of the Son, and of

и́мѧ твоѐ, Ѻ҆ц҃а̀, и҆ сн҃а, и҆ ст҃а́гѡ дх҃а, нꙑнѣ,
и҆ при́снѡ, и҆ во вѣ́ки вѣкѡ́въ.
Лю́дїе: А҆ми́нь.

И҆ и҆зше́дъ ст҃ꙑми две́рьми на соле́ю,
і҆ере́й зна́менꙋетъ лю́ди, глаго́лѧ:

И҆ да бꙋ́детъ бл҃года́ть и҆ ми́лость ст҃ꙑ́ѧ, и҆
є҆диносꙋ́щнꙑѧ, и҆ покланѧ́емꙑѧ трⷪ҇цꙑ со
всѣ́ми ва́ми.
Ли́къ: И҆ со дх҃омъ твои́мъ.

Дїа́конъ возглаша́етъ:

Со стра́хомъ бж҃їимъ во́нмемъ.

И҆ мо́литсѧ сщ҃е́нникъ,
глаго́лѧ ти́химъ гла́сомъ:

С҃те, во ст҃ꙑ́хъ почива́ѧй гдⷭ҇и, ѡ҆ст҃ѝ нꙑ
словомъ твоеѧ̀ бл҃года́ти и҆ наи́тїемъ
всест҃а́гѡ твоегѡ̀ дх҃а, тꙑ бо ре́клъ є҆сѝ,
влⷣко: ст҃и бꙋ́дите, ꙗ҆́коже а҆́зъ ст҃ъ є҆́смь,
гдⷭ҇ь бг҃ъ ва́шъ.

И҆ присовокꙋпла́етъ мл҃твꙋ сїю̀:

the Holy Spirit, now and ever, and unto the ages of ages.

SINGERS: Amen.

Coming out through the holy doors to the solea, the priest blesses the people, saying:

And may the grace and mercy of the holy, consubstantial, and adorable Trinity be with you all.

SINGERS: And with thy spirit.

The deacon exclaims:

With the fear of God, let us attend!

And the priest prays,
saying in a quiet voice:

O Holy Lord who restest in the holy place, make us holy by the word of Thy grace and by the visitation of Thine All-holy Spirit, for Thou hast said, O Master: 'Be holy, for I AM holy,' the Lord our God.

And he adds this prayer:

Не́нзрече́нне бж҃е сло́ве, ѻ҆ц7ꙋ и҆ прест7о́мꙋ дх҃ꙋ є҆диносꙋ́щне и҆ соприсносꙋ́щне и҆ нераздѣ́льне, прїими́ нетлѣ́ннꙋю пѣ́снь во ст7ы́хъ твои́хъ безкро́вныхъ же́ртвахъ съ хе́рꙋві̑мы и҆ серафі́мы и҆ ѿ менѐ грѣ́шнаго, вопїю́ща и҆ глаго́люща:

Возно́ситъ а́гнца по́дъ воздꙋ́хомъ, и҆ возглаша́етъ:

Преждешсц7е́нныѧ да́ры, ст7а́ѧ ст7ы́мъ.

Ли́къ ѿвеща́етъ:

Е҆ди́нъ ст7ъ, є҆ди́нъ гд7ь, і҆и7съ хр7то́съ, во сла́вꙋ бг7а ѻ҆ц7а̀. А҆ми́нь.

И҆ затворѧ́ютсѧ ст7ы́ѧ две́ри и҆ завѣ́са.

Дїа́конъ же, ста́въ на ѻ҆бы́чнѣмъ мѣ́стѣ, глаго́летъ проше́нїѧ сїѧ̑:

Рце́мъ всѝ ѿ сп7се́нїи, бл7гожи́тїи и҆ долгоде́нствїи ст7а́гѡ ѻ҆ц7а̀ на́шегѡ, а҆рхїепⷭ҇кѻпа (и҆ли́ митрополі́та) и҆́мк, всегѡ̀ при́чта и҆ хр7толюби́выхъ люде́й, и҆

O ineffable God and Word, consubstantial with the Father and the Holy Spirit, co-eternal and indivisible: accept this incorrupt hymn at Thy holy bloodless sacrifices with the Cherubim and the Seraphim, and also from me, a sinner, crying out and saying:

Then he elevates the Lamb
under the aer and exclaims:

Presanctified Gifts, Holy things unto the holies.

The singers respond:

One is holy, one is Lord, Jesus Christ, to the glory of God the Father. Amen.

The holy doors and the curtain are closed.

The deacon stands in the usual place
and says these petitions:

L et us all say for the salvation, good estate, and length of days of our holy father, Archbishop [or Metropolitan] N., of all the clergy and Christ-loving people, and

ѡ є҆́же ми́лостивꙋ и҆ бл҃гоꙋвѣ́тливꙋ бы́ти
бл҃го́мꙋ и҆ чл҃вѣколюби́вомꙋ бг҃ꙋ на́шемꙋ
ѡ грѣсѣ́хъ на́шихъ, и҆ поми́ловати ны по
вели́цѣй ми́лости чл҃вѣколю́бїа своегѡ̀, и҆
ѡ прости́тисѧ на́мъ всѧ́комꙋ прегрѣшѐнїю
во́льномꙋ же и҆ нево́льномꙋ, и҆ ѡ всѧ́кой
дꙋши̂ хрⷭ҇тїа́нстѣй, скорбѧ́щей же и҆
ѡѕло́бленнѣй, ми́лости бж҃їѧ и҆ по́мощи
требꙋ́ющей.

Ли́къ: Гдⷭ҇и поми́лꙋй.

Па́ки ѡ бг҃охрани́мѣй странѣ̀ се́й,
власте́хъ и҆ во́инствѣ є҆ѧ̀, и҆ ѡ є҆́же
и҆зба́вити лю́ди своѧ̑ ѿ вра̑гъ ви́димыхъ
и҆ неви́димыхъ, въ на́съ же ꙋ҆тверди́ти
є҆диномы́слїе, братолю́бїе и҆ бл҃гоче́стїе.

Ли́къ: Гдⷭ҇и поми́лꙋй.

И҆ ѡ сп҃се́нїи и҆ ѡставле́нїи грѣхѡ́въ
рабѡ́въ бж҃їихъ и҆́мⷬ҇къ, па́мѧти и҆ ꙋ҆покое́нїи
преподо́бныхъ ѻ҆тє́цъ на́шихъ и҆ бра́тїй, и҆
всѣ́хъ хрⷭ҇тїа́нъ правосла́вныхъ, рце́мъ всѝ.

Ли́къ: Гдⷭ҇и поми́лꙋй, в҃і.

that our good God who loves mankind may be gracious and favorable regarding our sins and may have mercy on us according to the great mercy of His love for mankind, and that every voluntary and involuntary sin may be forgiven us, and for every Christian soul that is afflicted and tormented, in need of mercy and help from God.

SINGERS: Lord have mercy.

Again for this God-preserved land, its authorities and armed forces, and that He may deliver His people from enemies visible and invisible, and confirm in us oneness of mind, brotherly love, and piety.

SINGERS: Lord have mercy.

And for the salvation and remission of the sins of the servants of God NN., the memory and repose of our venerable fathers and brothers, and of all Orthodox Christians, let us all say.

SINGERS: Lord, have mercy, 12.

Дїа́конъ: Въ ми́рѣ хр҃то́вѣ по́имъ. И вхо́дитъ
во ст҃ы́й ѻлта́рь.

Ли́къ же пое́тъ прича́стенъ:
ВкꙋсИ́те и ви́дите, ꙗ́кѡ бл҃гъ гд҃ь,
Аллилꙋ́їа, со стїха́ми ѱалма̀ л҃г,
Бл҃гословлю̀ гд҃а:

Ёгда̀ же глаго́летъ дїа́конъ прошє́нїа сїа̀,
сщ҃е́нникъ преломла́етъ ст҃ы́й хлѣ́бъ на
двѣ̀ ча́сти, и де́ржитъ десни́цею ча́сть и
шꙋ́йцею ча́сть. И раздробла́етъ
ст҃ы́й а҃гнецъ по ѻбы́чаю.

Пре́жде всѣ́хъ же, взе́мъ є҆ди́нꙋ ча́сть
ст҃а́гѡ хлѣ́ба, ꙗ́же І҃И҃С, влага́етъ ю̀ въ
ст҃ы́й поти́ръ, глаго́ла сло́во соединє́нїа:

Соединє́нїе прест҃а́гѡ тѣ́ла и ч҃тныа кро́ве
гд҃а и бг҃а и сп҃са на́шегѡ і҃и҃са хр҃та̀. Соедини́ся
и ѡсти́ся и соверши́ся во и҆́мꙗ ѻц҃а̀ и сн҃а
и ст҃а́гѡ дх҃а.

И па́ки глаго́летъ:

DEACON: **In the peace of Christ, let us sing.**
And he enters the holy sanctuary.

> The singers chant the communion verse
> **O taste, and see, that the Lord is good.**
> **Alleluia** with the verse of Psalm 33: **I will**
> **bless the Lord at all times . . .**

While the diaconal petitions were being
said, the priest breaks the Holy Bread in
twain, and holds each part in his right and
left hands. And he divides the holy Lamb
according to custom.

And first, taking one portion of the holy
Bread, i.e. IC, he places it into the holy
chalice, saying this prayer of the union:

The union of the most holy Body and the pre-
cious Blood of our Lord, God, and Saviour Je-
sus Christ. It has been united, and sanctified,
and fulfilled in the name of the Father and of
the Son and of the Holy Spirit.

> And again he says:

Се́ а҆́гнецъ бж҃їй, взе́млай грѣ́хъ мі́ра, закла́нный за мі́рскі́й живо́тъ и҆ спасе́нїе.

И҆ бл҃гословла́етъ сщ҃е́нникъ теплотꙋ̀ и҆ вливае́тъ ю҆̀ внꙋ́трь ст҃ы́а ча́ши по ѻ҆бы́чаю.

И҆ а҆́бїе раздробла́етъ ча́стицы ст҃а́гѡ хлѣ́ба, по ѻ҆бы́чаю, и҆ прїꙋготовла́етъ ча́стицы коемꙋ́ждо ѿ сослꙋжа́щихъ, глаго́ла:

Ча́сть ст҃а́а хрⷭ҇то́ва, и҆спо́лнена бл҃года́ти и҆ и҆́стины, ѻ҆ц҃а̀ и҆ сн҃а и҆ ст҃а́гѡ дх҃а, є҆мꙋ́же сла́ва и҆ держа́ва во вѣ́ки вѣко́въ.

Є҆гда̀ же прїꙋгото́витъ сщ҃е́нникъ ча́стицы во є҆́же причасти́ти сослꙋжа́щїа, глаго́летъ дїа́конъ:

Го́споди, бл҃гословѝ.

Сщ҃е́нникъ:

Бл҃гослове́нъ бг҃ъ, бл҃гословла́ай и҆ ѡ҆сща́ай

Behold, the Lamb of God, which taketh away the sin of the world, slain for the life of the world and its salvation.

And the priest blesses the hot water
and pours it into the chalice,
according to the custom.

And then he divides the particles of
the holy bread, according to the custom. And
he prepares the particles for each
of the concelebrants, saying:

The holy portion of Christ, full of grace and truth, of the Father, and of the Son, and the Holy Spirit, to whom belongs glory and power unto the ages of ages.

And after the priest prepares the particles
for the communion of the concelebrants,
the deacon says:

Lord, bless.

PRIEST:

Blessed is God who blesses and sanctifies us

на́съ и҆̀же во стра́сѣ бж҃їи раздробла́ющихъ
и҆ всѣ́хъ вѣ́рою причасти́тисѧ хота́щихъ
пречⷭ҇тыхъ та́инъ гдⷭ҇а и҆ бг҃а и҆ спⷭ҇а на́шегѡ
і҆и҃са хрⷭ҇та̀, ны́нѣ и҆ при́снѡ и҆ во вѣ́ки
вѣкѡ́въ.

И҆ ѿвѣща́ютъ всѝ клирі́ки: а҆ми́нь.

И҆ глаго́летъ млⷮ҇вꙋ сїю̀,
пре́жде ст҃а́гѡ причаще́нїѧ:

Е꙽А́кѡ хрⷭ҇тѐ бж҃е на́шъ, нбⷭ҇ный хлѣ́бе, пи́ще
всегѡ̀ мі́ра, согрѣши́хъ на нб҃о и҆ пре́дъ
тобо́ю, и҆ нѣ́смь досто́инъ причасти́тисѧ
ст҃ы́хъ и҆ пречⷭ҇тыхъ твои́хъ та́инъ, но
ра́ди бл҃гости твоеѧ̀ и҆ неизрече́ннагѡ
долготерпѣ́нїѧ, досто́йна мѧ̀ сотворѝ и҆
неѡсꙋжде́нна и҆ непостыдна причасти́тисѧ
престⷢ҇а́гѡ тѣ́ла и҆ чⷭ҇тныѧ кро́ве во ѡ҆ставле́нїе
грѣхѡ́въ и҆ въ жи́знь вѣ́чнꙋю.

Та́же творѧ́тъ по ѡ҆бы́чаю ст҃о́е
причⷭ҇тїе бж҃е́ственныхъ дарѡ́въ.

who in the fear of God are dividing the holy things, and all who with faith are about to partake of the most pure mysteries of our Lord, God, and Saviour Jesus Christ, now and ever, and unto the ages of ages.

And all clergy respond: **Amen.**

And the priest says this prayer, before the holy communion:

O Master Christ our God, the heavenly Bread, Food of the whole world, I have sinned before heaven and before Thee, and I am not worthy to partake of Thy holy and most pure mysteries, but for the sake of Thy goodness and Thine ineffable longsuffering, make me worthy, without condemnation or shame, to partake of Thy most holy Body and precious Blood unto the remission of sins and life everlasting.

Then the clergy receive the Holy Communion of the divine Gifts in accordance with the custom.

По причащенїи же сослꙋжа́щихъ, е҆гда́
же прїе́млетъ сщ҃е́нникъ ст҃ы́й дїскосъ,
глаго́летъ дїа́конъ: Го́споди, бл҃гословѝ.
Сщ҃е́нникъ: Сла́ва бг҃ꙋ, ѡ҆сти́вшꙋ и҆ ѡ҆сщ҃а́ющꙋ
на́съ.

И҆ па́ки глаго́летъ:

Вознеси́сѧ на нб҃еса̀, бж҃е, и҆ по все́й землѝ
сла́ва твоѧ̀, и҆ цр҃тво твое́ пребыва́етъ во
вѣ́ки вѣкѡ́въ, а҆ми́нь.

И҆ подае́тъ ст҃ы́й поти́ръ дїа́конꙋ, глаго́лѧ:
Бл҃гослове́но и҆́мѧ бг҃а на́шегѡ во вѣ́ки
вѣкѡ́въ.

Посе́мъ и҆схо́дитъ дїа́конъ съ ча́шею во
ст҃ы́ѧ две́ри, показꙋ́етъ ча́шꙋ лю́демъ
и҆ возглаша́етъ:

Со стра́хомъ бж҃їимъ и҆ вѣ́рою приступи́те.

Ли́къ же пое́тъ: Вкꙋси́те и҆ ви́дите,
ꙗ҆́кѡ бл҃гъ гдⷭ҇ь, а҆ллилꙋ́їа.

After the communion of the concelebrants,
when the priest takes the holy diskos,
the deacon says: Lord, bless.

PRIEST: Glory be to God who blesseth and
sanctifieth us.

And he says further:

Be Thou exalted above the heavens, O God,
and Thy glory above all the earth, and Thy
kingdom shall endure unto the ages of ages.
Amen.

Then he gives the holy chalice to the
deacon, saying: Blessed be the name of
our God unto the ages of ages.

Then the deacon goes out with the chalice
through the holy doors, shows the chalice
to the people, and exclaims:

With the fear of God and faith, draw nigh.

The singers chant: O taste, and see, that the
Lord is good. Alleluia.

Та́же пристꙋпа́ютъ хотѧ́щїе причаща́тисѧ,
и҆ причаща́ютсѧ по ѡ҆бы́чаю всѝ.

По причаще́нїи же, глаго́летъ дїа́конъ:

Го́споди, блгⷭ҇ови́.

Сщ҃е́нникъ же полага́етъ ст҃ꙋ́ю ча́шꙋ
на ст҃ꙋ́ю трапе́зꙋ и҆ глаго́летъ:

Сла́ва бг҃ꙋ, ѡ҆сти́вшꙋ всѣ́хъ на́съ. Бꙋ́ди и҆́мѧ
гдⷭ҇не блгⷭ҇ове́но во вѣ́ки.
Ли́къ: И҆спо́лни ᲂу҆ста̀ моѧ̀ хвале́нїѧ твоегѡ̀,
гдⷭ҇и, и҆ ра́дости и҆спо́лни ᲂу҆стнѣ̀ моѝ, ꙗ҆́кѡ
да воспою̀ сла́вꙋ твою̀. И҆лѝ и҆́ный тропа́рь
днѐ.

Сщ҃е́нникъ же блгⷭ҇овлѧ́етъ кади́ло,
прїе́млетъ кади́льницꙋ и҆ кади́тъ три́жды,
глаго́люще мл҃твꙋ кади́ла сїю̀:

В**озвесели́лъ ны е҆сѝ, бж҃е, въ соедине́нїи
твое́мъ, и҆ тебѣ̀ прино́симъ пѣ́снь
благода́рственнꙋю, пло́дъ ᲂу҆сте́нъ, и҆сповѣ́дающе благода́ть твою̀, съ кади́ломъ

Those to receive Communion draw near, and
partake according to the custom.

After communion, the deacon says:

Lord, bless.

And the priest places the chalice
upon the holy table and says:

Glory be to God who hath sanctified us all.
Blessed be the name of the Lord unto the
ages.

SINGERS: Fill my mouth with Thy praise, O
Lord, and fill my lips with joy, that I may sing
Thy glory. Or another troparion, as appropri-
ate for the day.

Meanwhile, the priest blesses the incense,
takes the censer and censes with it three
times, saying this prayer of the incense:

Thou hast made us glad, O God, in the union
with Thee, and with this incense do we offer unto Thee the song of thanksgiving, fruit of
the lips, confessing Thy grace. May it ascend

си́мъ: да взы́детъ пре́дъ тобо́ю, бж҃е, и̂ да не возврати́тсѧ вотщѐ, но дар́ꙋй и̂ на́мъ сегѡ̀ ра́ди бл҃гоꙋха́нїе прест҃а́гѡ твоегѡ̀ дх҃а, мѵ́ро пречи́стое и̂ неѿе́млемое, и̂спо́лни ꙋ̂ста̀ на́ша хвале́нїѧ, и̂ ꙋ̂стнѣ̀ ра́дованїѧ, и̂ се́рдце ра́дости и̂ весе́лїѧ.

Возглаше́нїе:

Ѿ хрⷭ҇тѣ̀ і̂и҃сѣ гдⷭ҇ѣ на́шемъ, съ ни́мже бл҃гослове́нъ є̂сѝ, и̂ со прест҃ы́мъ и̂ бл҃ги́мъ и̂ животворѧ́щимъ твои́мъ дх҃омъ, ны́нѣ и̂ при́снѡ и̂ во вѣ́ки вѣкѡ́въ.

Ли́къ: а̂ми́нь.

Бл҃годари́мъ тѧ, хрⷭ҇тѐ бж҃е на́шъ, ꙗ̂кѡ сподо́билъ є̂сѝ на́съ причасти́тисѧ пречи́стагѡ тѣ́ла и̂ честны́ѧ кро́ве смотре́нїѧ твоегѡ̀ въ жи́знь вѣ́чнꙋю. А̂ллилꙋ́їа (г҃-жды).

Сем́ꙋ же пѣва́ему, ѿхо́дѧтъ сщ҃е́нникъ и̂ дїа́конъ ко ст҃о́му предложе́нїю и̂ поставлѧ́ютъ та́мѡ ст҃а́ѧ. Та́же и̂зше́дъ и̂ ста́въ на ѡ̂бы́чнѣмъ мѣ́стѣ, дїа́конъ глаго́летъ:

before Thee, O God, and not return empty; but grant to us also the most pure myrrh that cannot be taken away, on account of this good fragrance of Thy Most Holy Spirit. Fill our mouths with praise, and our lips with rejoicing, and our heart with joy and gladness.

Exclamation:

In Christ Jesus, our Lord, with whom Thou art blessed, together with Thine All-holy, good, and life-giving Spirit, now and ever, and unto the ages of ages.

SINGERS: Amen.

We give thanks unto Thee, O Christ our God, that Thou hast made us worthy to partake of the most pure Body and precious Blood of Thy dispensation unto life everlasting. Alleluia (Thrice).

While this is sung, the priest and the deacon proceed to the table of oblation and place the holy Gifts there. Then, the deacon exits the sanctuary and, standing at the usual place, says:

Про́сти, прїи́мше ст҃ы́хъ, пречи́стыхъ, безсме́ртныхъ и҆ животворѧ́щихъ хрⷭ҇то́выхъ та́инъ во ѡ҆ставле́нїе грѣхẃвъ, досто́йнw бл҃годари́мъ гдⷭ҇а.

Ли́къ: Гдⷭ҇и, поми́лꙋй.

Ꙗ҆́кw да бꙋ́детъ на́мъ причаще́нїе ст҃ы́нь є҆гẁ во ѡ҆браще́нїе всѧ́кагw лꙋка́вагw дѣѧ́нїѧ, въ напꙋ́тїе живота̀ вѣ́чнагw, и҆ въ прича́стїе и҆ да́ръ ст҃агw дх҃а, помо́лимсѧ.

Ли́къ: Гдⷭ҇и, поми́лꙋй.

Прест҃ꙋ́ю и҆ пребл҃гослове́ннꙋю, пречи́стꙋю вл҃чцꙋ на́шꙋ бцⷣꙋ и҆ приснодв҃ꙋ мр҃і́ю со всѣ́ми ст҃ы́ми помѧнꙋ́вше, са́ми себѐ и҆ дрꙋ́гъ дрꙋ́га, и҆ ве́сь живо́тъ на́шъ хрⷭ҇тꙋ̀ бг҃ꙋ преддади́мъ.

Ли́къ: Тебѣ̀, гдⷭ҇и.

Сщ҃е́нникъ глаго́летъ
мл҃твꙋ сїю̀ та́йнw:

Бл҃годари́мъ тѧ̀, гдⷭ҇и бл҃гі́й и҆ стра́шный, ꙗ҆́кw оу҆таи́лъ є҆сѝ сїѧ̑ ѿ премꙋ́дрыхъ и҆ разꙋ́мныхъ, и҆ ѿкры́лъ є҆сѝ младе́нцємъ: є҆́й, о́ч҃е, ꙗ҆́кw та́кw бы́сть бл҃говоле́нїе

Aright! Having partaken of the holy, most pure, immortal, and life-giving mysteries of Christ for the remission of sins, let us worthily give thanks unto the Lord.

SINGERS: Lord have mercy.

That the communion of His holy things may be unto us for the repulsion of every evil deed, as a provision unto life everlasting, and for the communion and gift of the Holy Spirit, let us pray.

SINGERS: Lord have mercy.

Calling to remembrance our most holy, most blessed, most pure Lady Theotokos and Ever-Virgin Mary with all the saints, let us commit ourselves and one another and all our life unto Christ our God.

SINGERS: To Thee, O Lord.

The priest says this prayer secretly:

We give thanks to Thee, O good and fearsome Lord, for Thou hast hidden these things from the wise and prudent, and revealed them to babes: yea, Father, for

пред̾ тобо́ю. Ты̀ бо сподо́билъ є҆сѝ на́съ
воспрїа́ти тѣ́ло и҆ кро́вь є҆диноро́днагѡ сн҃а
твоегѡ̀, гд҃а на́шегѡ і҆и҃са хрⷭ҇та̀, мо́лимъ та̀
и҆ ми́лнса дѣ́емъ: да не во ѡ҆сꙋжде́нїе бꙋ́детъ
на́мъ причаще́нїе сїѐ, но во ѡ҆ставле́нїе
грѣхѡ́въ и҆ въ жи́знь вѣ́чнꙋю.

Возглаше́нїе:

Ꙗ҆́кѡ бл҃гослови́са и҆ ст҃и́са и҆ просла́вина
всест҃о́е и҆́ма твоѐ, ѻ҆ц҃а̀, и҆ сн҃а, и҆ ст҃а́гѡ дх҃а,
ны́нѣ, и҆ при́снѡ, и҆ во вѣ́ки вѣкѡ́въ.
Ли́къ: А҆ми́нь.
Сщ҃е́нникъ: Ми́ръ всѣ́мъ.
Ли́къ: И҆ дꙋ́хови твоемꙋ̀.
Дїа́конъ: Гла́вы̀ на́ша гдⷭ҇еви приклони́мъ.
Ли́къ: Тебѣ̀ гдⷭ҇и.

Сщ҃е́нникъ глаго́летъ мл҃твꙋ
главоприклоне́нїа та́йнѡ:

so it seemed good in Thy sight! For Thou hast made us worthy to receive the Body and Blood of Thine only-begotten Son, our Lord Jesus Christ, and we pray and entreat Thee: let this communion be not unto condemnation, but unto the remission of sins and life everlasting.

Exclamation:

For blessed, sanctified, and glorified is Thine All-holy name: of the Father, and of the Son, and of the Holy Spirit, now and ever, and unto the ages of ages.

SINGERS: Amen.

PRIEST: Peace be unto all.

SINGERS: And to thy spirit.

DEACON: Let us bow our heads unto the Lord.

SINGERS: To Thee, O Lord.

The priest says this prayer of inclination, secretly:

Б҃же и О́че гдⷭ҇а, и бг҃а и сп҃са на́шегш Іи҃са хрⷭ҇та̀, приклони́вый небеса̀ и сошéдый на сп҃сéнїе ро́да чл҃вѣ́ческагш, тебѣ̀ приклони́хомъ главы̀ на́ша, ѡ҆жидаю́ще твоегш̀ благословéнїа: прострѝ благодѣ́йственную ру́ку твою̀ и благословѝ всѧ̀ ны̀ благословéнїемъ дх҃о́внымъ.

Возглашéнїе:

Тебѣ̀ бо подобáетъ ѿ всѣ́хъ на́съ всѧ́кое славосло́вїе, чéсть, и поклонéнїе, О҆ц҃у̀, и сн҃у, и ст҃о́му дх҃у, нынѣ̀, и при́снш, и во вѣ́ки вѣкш́въ.

Ли́къ: А҆ми́нь.

Дїа́конъ: Въ ми́рѣ хрⷭ҇то́вѣ пои́мъ.

Ли́къ: Бу́ди и́мѧ гдⷭ҇не благословéно ѿ нынѣ̀ и до вѣ́ка. [Три́жды]

Сла́ва: и ны́нѣ.

И ѱало́мъ л҃г:

Благословлю̀ гдⷭ҇а:

Сщ҃éнникъ, и҆зшéдъ,
даéтъ лю́демъ а҆нтїдш́ръ.

O God and Father of our Lord, God, and Saviour Jesus Christ, who bowed down the heavens and came down for the salvation of the race of man, to Thee have we bowed down our heads, awaiting Thy blessing: stretch out Thy beneficent hand and bless us all with a spiritual blessing.

Exclamation:

For unto Thee is due from us all every doxology, honor, and worship: to the Father, and to the Son, and to the Holy Spirit, now and ever, and unto the ages of ages.

SINGERS: Amen.

DEACON: In the peace of Christ, let us sing!
SINGERS: Blessed be the name of the Lord from henceforth and forevermore. (Thrice)
Glory . . . Both now . . .

And Psalm 33:

I will bless the Lord . . .

The priest goes out and
distributes the antidoron.

По скончанїи же ѱалма̀, дїа́конъ
глаго́летъ:

Съ ми́ромъ и҆ любо́вїю бж҃їею и҆зы́демъ.
Ли́къ: И҆менемъ гдⷭ҇нимъ, влады́ко,
бл҃гословѝ.

И҆зше́дъ, сщ҃е́нникъ глаго́летъ мл҃твꙋ
ѿпꙋсти́тельнꙋю сїю̀ возгла́сно:

Оу҆пова́нїе всѣ́хъ концє́въ землѝ, хрⷭ҇тѐ
бж҃е, и҆́же зако́номъ и҆ прⷪ҇ро́ки и҆
бл҃говѣ́стники предвѣща́вый ст҃ы̑а твоѧ̑
дни̑ посто́въ ѡ҆чище́нїа и҆ сп҃се́нїа бы́ти
хода́тай, сподо́би и҆ на́съ всѣ́хъ тече́нїе поста̀
бл҃гопрїа́тно соверши́ти, вѣ́рꙋ неꙋкло́ннꙋ
соблюстѝ и҆ бж҃е́ствєнныѧ за́повѣди твоѧ̑
непоро́чно да́же до конца̀ сохрани́ти: а҆гг҃лꙋ
же ми́рнꙋ запове́ждь блюстѝ вхожде́нїа
на̑ша и҆ и҆схожде́нїа, и҆ стопы̀ оу҆тверди́ти
и҆ и҆спра́вити на пꙋтѝ ѡ҆правда́нїй твои́хъ:
прїе́млай же поста̀ и҆ колѣнопреклоне́нїа
на́шегѡ ст҃о́е вре́мѧ, возда́й на́мъ въ
бл҃гослове́нїихъ дх҃о́выхъ и҆ бл҃ги́хъ дарѣ́хъ, и҆

When the psalm is finished, the deacon says:

In peace and the love of God let us depart!
SINGERS: In the name of the Lord, master, bless!

The priest exits the altar and reads this prayer of the dismissal of the people, aloud:

O Christ our God, hope of all the ends of the earth, who through the Law, the prophets, and the evangelists didst foretell Thy holy days of the Fast to assist for our purification and salvation, do Thou also vouchsafe us all to complete the course of the Fast in an acceptable manner, to preserve the faith unshaken, and to keep Thy divine commandments blamelessly even until the end. Command an angel of peace to guard our comings in and our goings out, to confirm our steps and to direct them on the path of Thy statutes. Receiving the holy time of our fasting and kneeling, do Thou reward us with spiritual blessings and good gifts, and in the holy and

во ст҃е́мъ и҆ животворѧ́щемъ дни̑ воскрⷭ҇ні́ѧ
твоегѡ̀ сподо́би ны̀ твоегѡ̀ свѣ́та, ꙗ҆́кѡ
да хва́лимъ тѧ̀ є҆ди́нагѡ и҆́стиннагѡ бг҃а, и҆
тебѣ̀ сла́вꙋ и҆ бл҃годаре́нїе возсыла́емъ, ѻ҆ц҃ꙋ̀,
и҆ сн҃ꙋ, и҆ ст҃о́мꙋ дх҃ꙋ, нн҃ѣ и҆ при́снѡ, и҆ во
вѣ́ки вѣкѡ́въ.

Ли́къ: а҆ми́нь.

И҆ ѿхо́димъ во своѧ̑ си, бл҃годарѧ́ще бг҃а.

Коне́цъ бж҃е́ственныѧ лїтꙋргі́и
преждеѡсщⷩе́нныхъ дарѡ́въ ст҃а́гѡ сла́внагѡ
и҆ всехва́льнагѡ а҆пⷭ҇ла і҆а́кѡва бра́та гдⷭ҇нѧ.

life-giving day of Thy Resurrection make us worthy of Thy light, that we may praise Thee, the only true God, and may send up unto Thee glory and thanksgiving: to the Father, and the Son, and the Holy Spirit, now and ever, and unto the ages of ages.

SINGERS: Amen.

And we depart to our homes,
giving thanks to God.

End of the Divine Liturgy of the
Presanctified Gifts of the Holy,
Glorious and All-praised Apostle James,
Brother of the Lord.

BIBLIOGRAPHY

Ἡ Θεία Λειτουργία τοῦ ἁγίου Ἰακώβου τοῦ Ἀδελφοθέου. Jerusalem, 1912; 14th reprint: Athens, 2007.

The Divine Liturgy of the Holy Apostle James, the Brother of the Lord and First Hierarch of Jerusalem. Basking Ridge, NJ, 1978.

[Gardner, Philip, ed.] Божественная литургія св. апостола Іакова брата Божія и перваго іерарха Іерусалимскаго. Ladomirová: Brotherhood of St Job of Pochaev, 1938; reprint: Rome, 1970.

[Gardner, Philip] Общія указанія относительно чтенія Св. Писанія и пѣнія на Литургіи Св. Апостола Іакова. Приложеніе къ служебнику Литургіи Св. Апост. Іакова. Ladomirová: Printshop of St. Job of Pochaev, 1938.

[Gardner, Philip] *Руководство къ служенію Божественной литургіи святаго славнаго апостола Іакова брата Божія и перваго іерарха Іерусалимскаго.* Ladomirová: Printshop of St Job of Pochaev, 1939.

Kazamias, Alkiviades K. *Ἡ Θεία Λειτουργία τοῦ Ἁγίου Ἰακώβου τοῦ Ἀδελφοθέου καὶ τὰ νέα σιναϊτικὰ χειρόγραφα.* Thessalonica, 2006.

[Latas,] Archbishop Dionysios. *Ἡ Θεία Λειτουργία τοῦ ἁγίου ἐνδόξου ἀποστόλου Ἰακώβου τοῦ Ἀδελφοθέου καὶ πρώτου ἱεράρχου τῶν Ἱεροσολύμων, ἐκδοθεῖσα μετὰ διατάξεως καὶ σημεωσέων ὑπὸ Διονυσίου Λάτα, ἀρχιεπισκόπου Ζακύνθου.* Zakynthos, 1886.

Mercier, B.-Ch., ed. *La Liturgie de Saint Jacques. Édition critique du texte grec avec traduction latine.* Patrologia Orientalis 26.2. Paris, 1946.

Phountoulis, Ioannis M. *Θεία Λειτουργία Ἰακώβου τοῦ Ἀδελφοθέου.* Κείμενα Λειτουργικῆς 5. Thessalonica, 1977.

Phountoulis, Ioannis M. Λειτουργία τῶν προηγιασμένων δώρων Ἰακόβου τοῦ Ἀδελφοθέου. Κειμένα Λειτουργικῆς 19. Thessalonica, 1979.

Syrku, P. Къ исторіи исправленія книгъ въ Болгаріи въ XIV вѣкъ: литургическіе труды патріарха Евфимія Терновскаго. St Petersburg, 1890.

Tarchnishvili, Michel. *Liturgiae Ibericae Antiquiores.* 2 vols. CSCO 122-123. Louvain, 1950.

Xevsouriani, Lili, Stéphane Verhelst, et al. eds. *Liturgia Ibero-Graeca Sancti Iacobi. Editio – translatio – retroversio – commentarii.* Jerusalemer Theologisches Forum 17. Münster, 2011.